ST PETERSBURG

THE HIDDEN INTERIORS

ST PETERSBURG

THE HIDDEN INTERIORS

Katya Galitzine

Photography by
Leonid Bogdanov

With additional photography by
Oleg Trubsky & Pavel Demidov

HAZAR
P·U·B·L·I·S·H·I·N·G

For GG, with love

First published in 1999 by
Hazar Publishing Limited
147 Chiswick High Road,
London, W4 2DT

Design direction: Robert Mathias, Publishing Workshop
Designed by Helen Mathias

A catalogue for this title is available from the British Library.

Printed and bound in Great Britain by
Butler & Tanner Ltd, Frome and London

ISBN 1 874371 80 6

Acknowledgements

My grateful thanks for their continual help and support go to: my mother Jean
Galitzine, Ivan Bakhurin, Elena Konyukhova. Also to Andrei Dmitriev,
Stephen Raymond de Angelis, Zoya Chalova, Galina Popova, Andrei Bakhurin,
Anna Belorussova, Zakhar Kolovsky, Kyrill Zinoviev, Emanuel Galitzine, Philip
Goodman, special appreciation to Marie Clayton – my editor – for her incredible
patience, Leonid Bogdanov and also Valentina Golod for finding me the
wonderful Oleg Trubsky and Pasha Demidov.

For help with material and photographs in Russia I would like to thank:
Natalia Dementeeva, Vladimir Yakovlev, Boris Kirikov, Dmitry Butirin, Victor
Faibisovich, Yuri Ovseev, Marina Vershevskaya and Nadezhda Tikhonova,
Alexander Mylnikov, Nikolai Arnautov, Tamara Ivanova, Inna Lukotnikova, all
the staff at Oranienbaum, Janna Polyanaya and Tatyana Kniaseva, Vladimir
Zaitsev, Nikolai Kopanev, Evgeny Korchagin, Larisa Agmalian, Sergei
Nekrasov, Vladimir Bolshakov, Arkady Prokhanin, Ekaterina Grishina,
Alexander Sokolov and Larisa Sinitsyna, Tatyana Soloveva, Vladimir
Poludnyakov, Vladimir Sudulovsky at the St Petersburg Town Court, Angela
Brintlinger, Vyacheslav Makarov, Evgeny Kyichanov, Victor Kovalenkov, Lev
Vseviov, Zakhar Suponitsky, Nikolai Gviazdovsky, Janna Chistakova, Larisa
Zolotinsky-Freiman, Natalia Kuritzina, Svetlana Volchok, Svetlana Osipova and
Alexandra Kudriavtseva, Ivan Sautov and all the staff at Tsarskoe Selo, Anatoly
Ilin, Dmitry Solertinski, Alexander Brincken, Lama Shampa Dan'iot, Sergei
'Pit' Selivanov, Larisa Balashova, Tatyana Polova, Stephan Kaminski, Valentina
Demidova, Valentina Tyutcheva and Nelly Privalenko, Ludmilla Vydrina,
Captain Lev Chernavin, Tatyana Sukharnikova, Grigory Gaponov, Irena
Grintchenko, Pavel Gerasimov, Valera Krylov, Yuri Nagorvitsyn, Victor
Sharkov, Pavel Komsukaniants, Irena Chumerina, Sergei Buryachko, Leonid
Nadirov, Marina Vivien, all the Galinas at the Palaces of Weddings and
Malutka, Tatyana Makarova and Boris Igdalov plus the team of restorers for the
Amber Room, Anna Sukhorukova, Ivan Muvsyasyan, Misha Paltus, Nachalnik,
Renat, Nadia Ribinitskaya, Denis Kaché, Seva Gakell, Timor Novikov,
Georgie Guryanov, Oleg Maslov and Victor Kuznetzov, Aleksei and Andrei
Haas, Irena Davydov, Inna Karachunskaya, everyone at 46 Fontanka, Maria
Timofeevna Litovchenko and the Anikushin family.

Transliteration of Russian names checked by Dr Nathan Franklin Longan,
Assistant Professor for Russian Language & Literature, Oakland University,
Detriot, USA

Author's Note

There can be no correct solution to the transliteration of Russian names,
although there are several accepted systems. We have tried to be consistent, but
rather than sticking rigidly to one system in some cases we have used familiar
forms. As to my family name, nowadays it is often transliterated as Golitsyn but
we use Galitzine, which is the phonetic French version adopted by members of
the family in the Corps Diplomatique in the 18th century and which has been
accepted as traditional in the family.

FRONTISPIECE: *The Knights Hall in the former mansion of the Polish Count Peter
Ivanovich Paskevich-Erevansky, on the English Embankment. The building was decorat-
ed in Gothic style towards the end of the 19th century by architects Pelle and Gegike.
The mansion also has a Winter Garden, an Oak Buffet, a Gothic Hall and a Swan
Hall, and once housed a first-class art collection.*

TITLE PAGE: *The coat of arms of the Paskevich-Erevansky family once sported sea-faring
images, but was redesigned in Soviet times with the hammer and sickle and head of
Lenin. Before the economic crisis of 1998 the house was being restored to its former
glory, sponsored by a bank which leased the building as offices.*

CONTENTS

INTRODUCTION

I first went to Leningrad in 1985 and found a magical city, full of contrasts. I began living there in 1989, exploring my roots and the changing Soviet culture amidst St Petersburg's beautiful Imperial architecture. It was a strange time – there was nowhere else like it in the world. Grandiose facades hid the final muddled moments of the Communist regime, people bursting with new ideas filled empty rooms, domestic traditions created warm stability at a time when rules were demanding to be challenged. I was in my element and I met extraordinary people – brave and excited by the coming changes, imaginative, flexible, and passionate. I discovered secret places that had been closed or misused for years, layers of wallpaper that peeled away to reveal the story of the 20th century. The dissolution of Communism caused yet more excitement and we all rode on a wave of hope for the next five years. St Petersburg, as it became again, was vibrant, filled with energy from both past and present. In Moscow, parliamentary and economical reforms were taking place but 'Peter's City', as its founder had intended, was a city of dreams. Gradually, the realities of the new democracy crept up from the capital and into the lives of the romantic 'Petersburgers'. The one constant that remained amidst these changes were the buildings, the walls within which so much creativity and agitation had existed.

St Petersburg holds a fascination for everyone. Hidden behind doors are historians, scientists, aristocrats, poets, sportsmen, collectors, tailors, musicians – all with a story to tell, a different reality, a new view. Sometimes, when I am sitting with Romanov fanatics, I imagine I am in a ghost town, filled only with memories, myths and decaying palaces. Two nights later, in a bar with trendy, attractive artists, I listen to plans for a bright, new future. Sitting over cups of tea with shaking heads are those who still miss the Communist regime – how well they remember the good old days when everything seemed to be clean and in order. Most important are the workers, who have so far kept the mechanism of the city running despite every change. One thing that cannot be doubted is the pride that Russians have for their country, and the extra-special love that St Petersburg invokes. For in whatever period she has always been magnificent, whether in suffering or triumph, in excess or deprivation. Europeans, Americans, Ukrainians, Moslems – all find something that charms them into loving this town. When living here, I fall under the spell of the Russian culture and morality; I am driven by deeper emotions and a different sense of necessity. The Russian character naturally leaves much to Fate and the pleasure of relaxing in good company counts for more than the satisfaction of achievement. Life becomes very calm and enjoyable.

Three men helped me fall in love with this city. Primarily my father, George

Galitzine, (1916-1992), who loved Russia despite all it had done to his family. He taught me about pre-Revolutionary Russian history and encouraged my love of beautiful architecture. Mikhail Anikushin, (1917-1997), my teacher, who as an artist showed me the strengths within the Soviet system and in his wisdom rode the wave of change. Finally my friend, Sergei Kuryokhin, (1953-1996), who revealed the future of St Petersburg and encouraged me to be bold and go through closed doors. I am grateful to them for introducing me to different aspects of the city. There are also all my friends who have helped me through the years; introducing me to new viewpoints and keeping me intrigued. However, it is my own 'Alice-like' curiosity that has added the final dimension to this collage – I like to open doors and find out what lies behind them. It is a habit I picked up from my father who, decades earlier, would enter unknown places with grace and charm and often find himself embarking on an unexpected private guided tour. I wish he was alive to read this book, he would have loved investigating the stories of these previously unexplored places.

I hope the places I have included in this book will illustrate the history of the city from a different angle. St Petersburg through its glory, its tradition, its wars and scandals and finally the transformation of the 20th century, whether under the Soviets or by the new capitalists now claiming the town. Together with the history there are sketches of events, people and atmosphere that should conjure up new images of this multi-faceted city. Visiting the locations has offered countless experiences, a book in itself. A mix of bureaucracy and diplomacy achieved access to most places, but we then had to adjust to the temperament of the staff; some have been casual, some formal, some disinterested, some over-keen to help – all, without exception, love 'their' houses.

Some of the buildings I have visited in this book may be well known from the outside, others are almost unknown even to Russians, a great majority have rarely, if ever, been photographed. It has been very difficult to make a final selection. Being the former capital of Russia, St Petersburg has a rich and varied heritage and such a diversity of places that it would be impossible to include them all. Every building, every period, has its own expert, with a fund of information that would fill a book on its own. A historical town always has its fair share of historians, and there are many people in St Petersburg with unpublished books in drawers who know far more than I have been able to include about some of my choices. I feel very privileged to be able to introduce my own small selection of the hidden interiors of St Petersburg. My own life has obviously influenced the inclusion of a number of places, the various insider views that I have been lucky to experience. Although I was brought up in England, I have spent my formative adult years mainly in St Petersburg watching my contemporaries and friends graduate from the 'underground' to principal roles in the city's cultural engine.

I have approached this project as I would a sculpture, but my materials have been words and historical facts and the object has been to build a portrait of St Petersburg. The book has developed in several stages: my innocent investigation of the city played an important part in the accumulation of information over the years; the organization of the photography and the factual research; and finally the writing and compiling.

So much Russian history is being rediscovered and unearthed. This book only touches the surface, for St Petersburg is full of hundreds more treasures, the backdrop to tragic or romantic tales. As more of the recently-opened archives are studied and published, more ghosts are released into a city that is still struggling to find its 20th-century identity. Meanwhile the story lives on behind closed doors.

KATYA GALITZINE, ST PETERSBURG 1999

LEFT: *Katya's desk.*

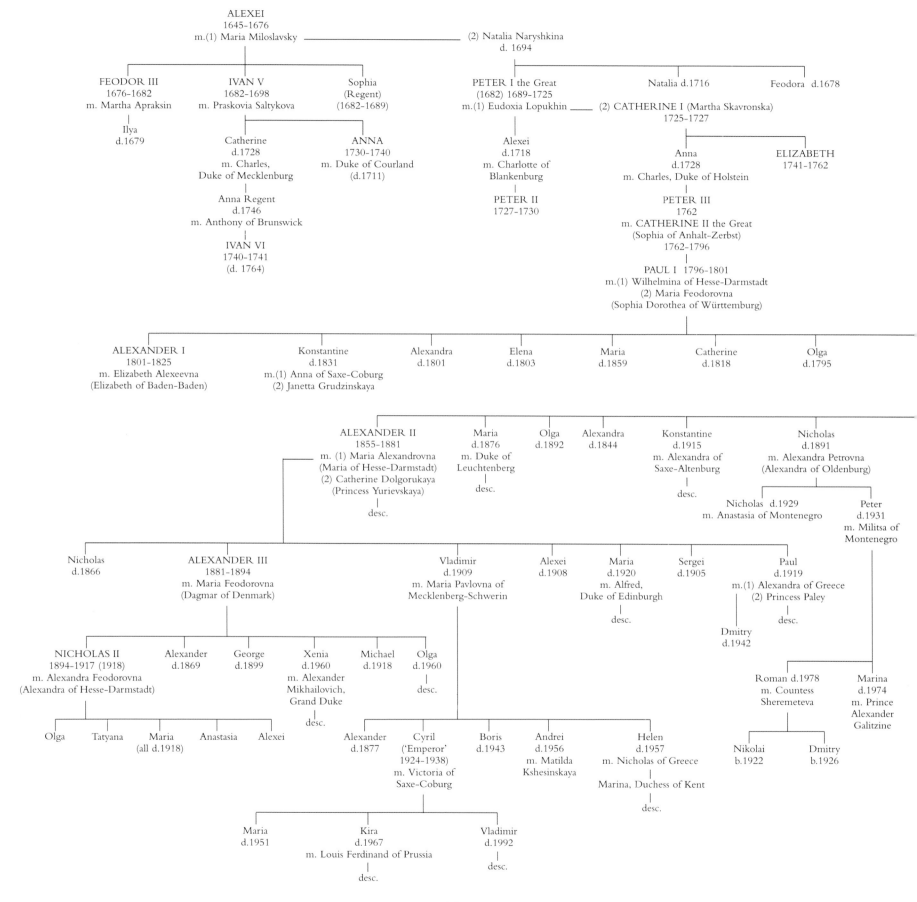

FAMILY TREE

The Romanov dynasty began in 1613 when the Zemsky Sobor, an assembly of boyars, gentry and clergy, ended the Time of Troubles and placed 16-year-old Mikhail Romanov on the throne. After Paul I, the Romanov line passed only through the male heir. From then on the title Grand Duke/Duchess was given exclusively to children or grandchildren of the Tsar, but the title Prince/Princess denoted a member of the old nobility. Count and Baron were translations from the German and were titles bestowed from the time of Peter the Great. The princely family of Galitzine is descended from the first King of Lithuania, Gedemine (d.1341). It can also be spelt Golitsyn and, apart from the Dolgorukys, no other family appears more frequently in Russian history.

LEFT: The author's family, shortly after their escape from Russia: Catherine with George (the author's father) and Emanuel, Natalia Countess Carlow, Nicholas, Maria and her son, Dmitry.

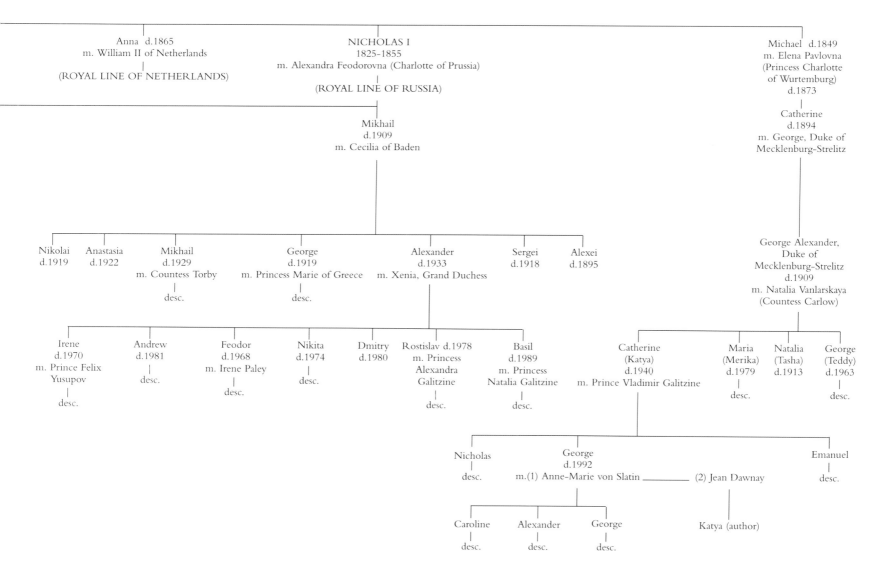

Key to map of St Petersburg

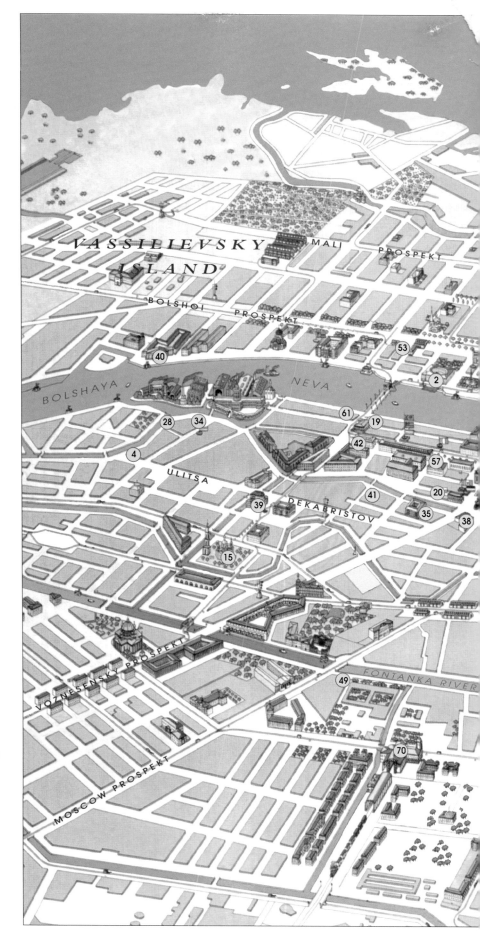

1. 46 Fontanka
2. Academy of Arts
3. *Admiralty*
4. Alexander Blok's Apartment
5. Alliluyev Apartment
6. Anichkov Palace
7. *Anikushin's Studio*
8. Artillery Museum
9. Aurora
10. *Bank*
11. Boiler Room
12. Botanical Gardens
13. Buddhist Temple
14. Casino
15. Cathedral of St Nicholas of the Sea
16. Central Archives
17. Circus
18. *City Court*
19. DK Mayak
20. Dom Architects
21. Dom Officers
22. Dom Radio
23. Eliseev
24. Elizarov Apartment
25. Ethnographic Museum
26. Fish Fabrique
27. Geographic Institute
28. *Grand Duke Alexei*
29. Grand Hotel Europe
30. Institute of Electricity
31. Kirov's Apartment
32. Kshesinskaya Mansion
33. Kunstkammer
34. Lesgaft Sports Institute
35. Lombard
36. Malutka
37. Market
38. Mariinsky Palace
39. Mariinsky Theatre
40. Mining Institute
41. Montferrand
42. Moorish Room/ Grand Duke Nicholas
43. Moorish Room/ Grand Duke Vladimir
44. Mukhinskaya Academy of Art
45. Museum of the Arctic & Antarctica
46. Naval Museum
47. Nekrasov's Apartment
26. New Academy
48. *New Mikhailovsky Palace*
49. Old Cafe
50. Palace Bridge
51. Palace of Weddings
52. Peter's Summer Palace
53. Pharmacy
54. Philharmonia
55. Planetarium
56. *Polovtsov Dacha*
57. Post Office
58. Printing Museum
59. Pushkin's Apartment
60. Pyramid Disco
61. Rumiantsev Palace
62. Russian National Library
63. St Isaac's Cathedral
64. Sheremetev Palace
65. Stone Island Palace
66. Telephone Exchange
67. Trubetskoy Bastion of the Peter & Paul Fortress
68. University
69. *Vaganova School*
70. Vitebsky Station
71. Yusupov Palace on Liteiny

ADDITIONAL LOCATIONS NOT ON MAP:

1,000,000 Club – on Stachek Square, south-west of the city centre

Alexander Palace – next to the Catherine Palace at Tsarskoe Selo, 15km south of St Petersburg

Amber Room – in the Catherine Palace at Tsarskoe Selo

Avtovo metro station – on the Kirovsko-Vyborgskaya metro line, south of main city centre

Birch Pavilion – in the grounds of Gatchina, 45km south-west of St Petersburg

Imperial Lycée – attached to the Catherine Palace at Tsarskoe Selo, 15km south of St Petersburg

Katalnaya Gorka – in the grounds of Oranienbaum, 29km west of St Petersburg

Kirov Factory – south-west of the main city centre, on the road to Peterhof

Oranienbaum – 29km west of St Petersburg, on the Gulf of Finland

Priyutino – 30km east of St Petersburg

Pulkhovo Observatory – south of St Petersburg, beyond the airport

Rose Pavilion – in the grounds of Pavlovsk, 30km south of St Petersburg

Smolny Institute – east of the city centre, next to Smolny Cathedral

St Sergius Monastery – in Strelna, on the road to Peterhof

Locations in italics are not generally open to the public.

CREATION OF A CITY

FOUNDED BY PETER THE GREAT, St Petersburg was an ambitious project to create a port for his empire, the legendary 'Window on the West'. In 1703 he began building on the marshy banks of the Neva, battling against floods, fire and the wolves roaming the area. During the construction, thousands of workmen lost their lives. In 1712, after the Russian victory at the Battle of Poltava, Peter decided that his new city was now strong enough to become the capital of Russia, so all his nobles were obliged to build houses in the area.

The original city was based on islands divided by canals – an attempt by Peter to recreate Amsterdam. European architects were commissioned to establish the outline of the new capital, with most buildings designed in a plain and simple style. During this period a few summer residences also began to spring up just outside St Petersburg along the shores of the Gulf of Finland. Later, in the reign of Peter's daughter, Elizabeth, the architecture developed a more fanciful style as the blue and white Baroque buildings known as Elizabethan Rococo emerged.

When Catherine the Great arrived in St Petersburg the city was made of wood, when she left it was built in stone. Catherine introduced enlightened ideas and reforms from Europe, just as Peter had imported architects, craftsmen and engineers. She created a distinction between public and private architecture and, influenced by the European revival of the Classical style, built many new buildings during her reign. It was no longer necessary to force the nobility to take up residence in St Petersburg – many recognized the signs of a maturing Western society and flocked to the capital to be part of it.

ADMIRALTY

The golden spire of the Admiralty is a central landmark of St Petersburg; from it stem the main arteries of the city, Nevsky Prospekt, Middle Prospekt (now Ulitsa Gorokhovaya) and Voznesensky Prospekt. Rising 72m (230 feet) from a square Classical tower, its glint dominates the city. The northern sun sets behind it, creating a beautiful silhouette that is instantly recognizable as St Petersburg.

When the city was founded, the Admiralty site was a shipyard, with docks and a wharf. Peter the Great's intention was to build a port into Europe from Russia – the much quoted 'Window on the West'.

The Admiralty building was designed by A.D. Zakharov and built between 1806 and 1823. Zakharov died in 1811, never to see his great work completed. His original design included a wide moat allowing ships to come and go; he integrated the main canals of the shipyard to flow under the two side pavilions facing the Neva. An original tower on the site, built by I.K. Korobov, was encased with the present quadrangle tower. Today, (with special permission) one can climb to the attic and see the inner layer of brickwork with its wooden beams surrounded by Zakharov's grand windowless encasement, and, even higher, stand amidst the white columns to admire the most magnificent view of the city.

The Naval Museum was based in these buildings before the Revolution, and here was the last, weak defence of the Tsarist force in February 1917. During the Second World War, a hot air balloon carried mountaineers to the top of the golden spire, with its weather vane in the shape of a ship, to camouflage it with sackcloth. Despite this, the Admiralty complex received five, hugely damaging, direct hits by bombs and 20 missiles. Most of the interiors were destroyed, including the plafond by G.B. Scotti in the White Column Hall, but a few of the Classical rooms have since been restored. The Admiralty buildings are now the headquarters for the St Petersburg Naval Base, and also house the Dzerzhinsky Higher Naval Engineering Academy. Both were top-secret Soviet establishments dealing with defence, so only a few know what the Admiralty looks like within. It remains just a beautiful façade for both residents and visitors alike.

OPPOSITE PAGE: *The main staircase and central Entrance Hall. The upper level is lined with post-war busts of famous Russian admirals.*

ABOVE: *Most of the Admiralty has lost its Classical decor. The Admiralty church later became a recreation hall.*

LEFT: *In 1992, the Library caught fire and suffered extensive damage from the water used to extinguish the flames – the faux marble is now peeling and the wood fittings have warped.*

TRUBETSKOY BASTION

LEFT: *The Trubetskoy Bastion was opened as a museum in 1924. A board outside each door tells the visitor which revolutionary occupied which cell, but they fail to give information about prisoners other than Bolsheviks. Cell 60 was occupied by Maxim Gorky in 1905, and by Prince Nikolai D. Galitzine for a week in 1917.*

O n May 27, 1703, Peter the Great sliced two strips of turf with his sword, laid them on the ground in a cross, and declared the foundation of his city, St Petersburg. Within seven months, using forced labour and Swedish prisoners, the first version of the Peter & Paul Fortress stood on the spot Peter had selected, on Hare's Island at the widest part of the Neva estuary. The walls were of earth and wood, but Domenico Trezzini – the first architect of the city – later replaced them with 4m thick brick covered with granite slabs. The fort was built in a six-point shape, with

BELOW LEFT: *A cell, restored to its 19th-century appearance, shows what conditions were like for political prisoners in Imperial Russia. All the cells were damp and cold, but some located below the level of the Neva were permanently flooded. Prisoners suffered from TB and scabies, and were kept in solitary confinement – the lack of human contact often led to suicide or madness.*

bastions defending each corner named after Peter and five of his generals: Menshikov, Naryshkin, Golovkin, Zotov and Trubetskoy. The Trubetskoy Bastion became the most famous political prison of Tsarist Russia; the first victim to be imprisoned within its walls was Peter's son Alexei, who was supposedly beaten to death by his father's own hand.

Later, the Secret House was built by Empress Anna – a maximum security prison on Alexeevsky Ravelin, for those who questioned Romanov authority. It was here that the Decembrists were incarcerated, before being tried in the Commandant's House. Dostoevsky was also imprisoned here for being part of the Petrashevsky Circle – he was led out to be executed but reprieved at the last minute, a scene he immortalized in *The Idiot*.

In 1872, the Secret House was demolished and the Trubetskoy Bastion again became the main prison. It contained 69 identical cells, each furnished with a bed, table, and stool, with asphalt floors and windows with iron bars set high in the fortress walls. The cells were soundproofed – the walls were covered in stretched canvas, hiding metal chains hung between two layers of felt to stop prisoners communicating by banging on pipes. If they were caught trying to communicate, the punishment was solitary confinement in total darkness. The special green-cloaked guard wore felted shoes, so they could creep up the long corridors and spy through the door slits.

In the 1880s, terrorists from 'Land and Liberty' and 'The People's Will' (Alexander II's assassins), were held here. Alexander Ulianov was imprisoned and executed for plotting against the Tsar; after his death, all his younger siblings became revolutionaries, determined to have their revenge – one of them was Lenin. After the 1905 Revolution, Maxim Gorky was held, as was Trotsky, who insisted on wearing a smart evening suit. In 1917 the prison was subject to an abrupt about-turn: first revolutionaries were imprisoned – the Pavlovsky Regiment (19 to a cell) who had refused to fire at citizens – and later their former guards when the regiment became Heroes of the Revolution and were freed. The Provisional Government arrested their counterparts – Prince Nikolai D. Galitzine, President of the Tsar's Government and a rather frail man of 65, spent a week in cell 60. After the Bolshevik take-over, members of the Provisional Government and the Imperial family were held here and Grand Dukes

LEFT: *Once people were reluctant to go near the Peter & Paul Fortress walls – now they rush there in the summer months, as the banks outside are a popular spot for sunbathers.*

BELOW: *A recreation of the Tribunal Hall in the Commandant's House, which was used for major political trials. Nicholas I personally participated in the trials of the 289 Decembrists in 1826, condemning five leaders to death and 31 to imprisonment, while the rest were banished to Siberia. When the leaders of the revolt were hanged at the Kronverk, three of the ropes broke – but the prisoners were not reprieved, as was the custom in those days.*

Nikolai Mikhailovich, Paul Alexandrovich, George Mikhailovich and Dmitry Konstantinovich were among those shot against the fortress walls in January 1919. The bastion was last used in 1921, to hold sailors from Kronstadt, who had mutinied against the Communists.

PETER'S SUMMER PALACE

Along the leafy avenues of the Summer Garden, where the Fontanka meets the Neva, stands a two-storey yellow stucco house. This modest summer residence of Peter the Great, and his consort Catherine, was built by Domenico Trezzini in 1710. In contrast to the grandness of the gardens, which were intended to imitate Versailles, the little brick house contained a simple Dutch interior.

In the early 18th century, Peter's apartments were on the ground floor, where he had a carpentry workshop. He enjoyed donning a leather apron and using his lathe, and would often receive guests in such a pose. The walls of this room are lined with paintings of sea views. A large German instrument for measuring the wind was attached to the St George weathervane on the roof; Peter could therefore always tell whether the sea was rough or calm, and how his ships were faring.

Peter was excluded from Court life as a young boy by his half-sister, Sophia, and her lover Prince Vassily Galitzine. He lived with his mother, Natalia Naryshkina, in Preobrazhensky outside Moscow near a German colony. Peter's education was mainly through his own curiosity and experimentation and he loved visiting the carpenter, blacksmith, joiner and printer and trying out their trades with his own hands. He learnt several crafts, his favourite being shipbuilding, which he studied at Zaandam in Holland and Deptford in England in 1698.

My heart's with the roses, in my beloved grounds
Which my beloved wrought iron fences surround,
Where statues remember me as a young girl,
And I, Nevan floodwaters over them swirl,
In silence and fragrance, among regal limes
I fancy I hear ship masts creaking, sometimes.
A swan seems to float through the aeons, as before,
Bewitched by his double's magnificent form.
Asleep in the gardens are steps without end
Of friends and of foes, of foes and of friends.
And there is no end to the columns of wraiths
That stretches from granite vase to palace gates.
There, gentle wind whispers at night, high above,
Of somebody's secret and exalted love.
And all things are lit by a nacreous glow –
The source of the light is a mystery, though.

ANNA AKHMATOVA

LEFT: *Catherine's Reception Room has walls lined in green silk. When she ascended the throne after Peter's death, all receptions took place in this palace according to Court etiquette, and this room led into the Red Presence Room or Throne Room.*

OPPOSITE PAGE: *The Summer Garden is one of the most romantic places in the city.*

BELOW: *The kitchen, with its Dutch ceramic tiles, has remained intact since Peter's day. A black marble wash-basin was supplied with the first running water system in St Petersburg. Peter invented a hatch in the wall in order to have his meals served hot, directly from the stove.*

The atmosphere in his palace was very informal; he surrounded himself with visiting sailors, his friends and the weird collection of followers gathered on his journeys. He enjoyed merrymaking and forced those around him to participate in heavy drinking sessions and crude jokes. Catherine, his Livonian wife, lived on the second floor with their children and was often called upon by unlucky guests to soothe the Tsar's fiery temper. There is an apocryphal story about how they met: Catherine was one of Menshikov's camp followers, a laundress whose strong hands could massage away the pains in Peter's head. For this, and her honest, humble qualities, he fell in love with her, married her and made her Empress.

The palace is only 400sqm, but was cleverly proportioned to accommodate Peter's 2m height. It seems tremendously light, due to the large collection of mirrors placed opposite windows. Mirrors were great luxuries – as was glass, and the windows of the Summer Palace are made up of many small

panes. The kitchens were plumbed with running water from the Summer Garden – at that time filled with fountains fed from the neighbouring river, which was therefore named the Fontanka.

ABOVE: *Chinese silk lines the walls of the Dancing Room, where Peter's young daughters, Anna and Elizabeth, were trained to dance..*

LEFT: *Peter loved ships and covered the walls of his favourite rooms with sea views. His first collection of curiosities was housed in special fitted cupboards in the Summer Palace.*

RIGHT: *The huge Tsar slept upright in a bed half his size, propped up by pillows. Doctors believed this would stop the blood rushing to his head and cure him of headaches. The walls are covered with printed velvet and the ceiling is painted with the god of sleep, Morpheus, scattering poppies. Above the stove is a moulded figure of a boy on a dolphin, believed to be the work of Andreas Schlüter.*

The Summer Garden, with its avenues lined with Classical sculpture, is witness to St Petersburg's history; the trees planted by Peter are as old as the city itself. During Catherine the Great's time, an elegant set of wrought iron railings was added, designed by Velten. Tchaikovsky's opera, *The Queen of Spades* opens in the playful context of the Garden. Under the sidelong gazes of white marble statues, the shady paths are still the courting grounds of lovers, young and old. Perhaps the enthusiasm with which Peter created his 'kitchen garden' has instilled an aura of happiness here.

UNIVERSITY

On the Neva Embankment of Vassilievsky Island are the long buildings that house the University. They are some of the earliest constructions in the city, built by Domenico Trezzini and his son, Guiseppe, and completed after Peter the Great's death. The flat decorations and two colours of the façade are typical of Peter's time, but inside the only original interiors remaining are the Western Gallery, by Trezzini, and the plasterwork and fireplaces in the Petrovsky Hall, by Ignacio Rossi – father of Carlo.

The University consists of 12 two-storey buildings, each with its own roof. The subject for Russia's first architectural competition, they were originally built for the Government Senate. There is an apocryphal story about them; Menshikov – Peter's childhood friend and sparring partner, had already started to build his own palace slightly further along the embankment. Due to the continual rivalry between him and Peter he wanted his house to be the primary stone building in the area. While Peter was abroad, very busy and unable to control the construction works, Menshikov was put in charge. He therefore ordered that the new building should face east (sideways from the river), and when Peter returned it was too late to change anything!

It was not until 1835 that the ministries moved to Senate Square and the University was fully established. The original ground floor was an arcade of shops, which was redeveloped

Dmitry Ivanovich Mendeleev

Dmitry Ivanovich Mendeleev, the famous Russian chemist, was born in 1834 in Tobolsk, the 17th child of a provincial family. After qualifying as a teacher and winning a gold medal for academic achievements, he obtained an advanced degree in chemistry at the University in 1856. In 1864 he became Professor of Chemistry at the Technical Institute, and three years later was made Professor of General Chemistry at the University. Since he could not find a textbook that met his needs, he set about writing his own; the result was The Principles of Chemistry *(1868-70), a classic textbook. Mendeleev formulated the* Periodic Law, *which shows the relation of elements when arranged in increasing atomic weight order. In his final version of the* Periodic Table *(1871) he left gaps, foretelling that they would be filled by elements not then known and predicting the properties of three of those elements.*

LEFT: *Original heating stove from 1736, designed by Ignacio Rossi, in the corner of the Petrovsky Hall.*

FAR LEFT: *Mendeleev's study at the University. He was not simply a 'mad genius', he was also a very practical man – as is shown in his ordered filing system in the Library in his apartments at the University. Mendeleev headed the Bureau of Weights and Measures and set up a new system of import duties on heavy chemicals.*

BELOW: *One of the few examples of original plasterwork from Peter the Great's time, in the Petrovsky Hall.*

with windows by A.F. Shchedrin when the University needed more facilities. Shchedrin changed almost all the interiors, creating the marble staircase that leads to a large hall with white columns – where graduation ceremonies are still held – and the University Church.

The St Petersburg (or Leningrad) University has educated and employed some of the greatest Russian minds: Lomonosov, Dostoevsky, Pavlov, Tchaikovsky, Blok, Joseph Brodsky, Dmitry Likhachev, to name but a few. With the development of the sciences new facilities were created, including an observatory and a chemistry laboratory at the end of the 19th century, and computer programming facilities more recently.

ABOVE: *Shelves displaying samples of chemicals in Mendeleev's study.*

OPPOSITE PAGE: *The Gallery designed by Trezzini (1737-41) along the western façade of the premier building. The long corridor is lined with portraits of famous graduates and doors opening onto classrooms.*

KUNSTKAMMER

Founded in 1718 by Peter the Great, the Kunstkammer was the first museum in St Petersburg. Peter wanted to introduce 'culture' to the people and exhibit some of the curios that he loved to collect on his travels, but his idea of culture was slightly eccentric; the new museum exhibited freaks (both live and bottled) and unusual skeletons, which he would set up in contorted positions for his own amusement. Also on show was his personal dental equipment, since he had a penchant for removing other people's teeth, and the remains of his friend, Bourgeois the giant — who, along with other degenerates and freaks, had been encouraged to come and live in St Petersburg. The new museum was built around a deformed pine tree (part of which is on display today) and

Peter encouraged visitors to the museum by promising a shot of vodka or wine at the end of their tour.

The museum still contains items from Peter's original collection, although in 1747 a fire destroyed much of the building, including the distinctive tower built by Chiaveri. Some 200 years later the tower was rebuilt, and it now houses the unusual globe presented to Peter by a Count of Gothorp. Inside the globe are painted illustrations of a starry sky and mythical gods of the heavens and sea; ten people can sit inside and it rotates. Although the globe was also burnt in the fire, it was rebuilt in the 18th century. After 1917, it was moved to Pushkin, where it remained until the Nazis took it to Germany as a war trophy. In 1946, the globe was found in

Lübeck and returned to the Kunstkammer.

During the reign of Alexander II, the collection was redistributed to the Zoological, Mineralogical, Botanical and Anthropological museums. In 1913, to celebrate 300 years of the Romanov dynasty, the Kunstkammer was named in memory of Peter the Great and much of the collection was returned. In Soviet times, the most precious items – the Scythian gold, Rembrandts, Peter's study and wax image – were moved to the Hermitage.

Alaska was still Russian in the 18th century, and Russian explorers visited California and collected rare objects from Native Americans (still known as Red Indians in Russia, even today), such as a Sioux chieftain's cloak of parrot feathers. The huge image of a Ceylonese demon, which once stood at the entrance to a temple, and a Vietnamese God of Hunters were presents to Nicholas II when he was Tsarevich. Also in the collection are pickled foetuses in bottles decorated with lace, which were fashionable on ladies' dressing tables in the late 18th century.

In the original museum to the left of the entrance was a stuffed elephant. Krylov's fable, *The Sightseer* (1814), is about someone who visits the museum and describes every room in detail – but forgets to mention the large beast. 'Krylov's Elephant' is now an analogy in Russian for overlooking the obvious.

OPPOSITE PAGE: *In the 19th century, a surgeon would dissect corpses in the Round Hall whilst visitors watched from the galleries above.*

RIGHT: *Recreation of Lomonosov's study, with some of his original instruments. Lomonosov was a 'Renaissance Man' during the reign of Catherine the Great.*

ABOVE TOP: *The round table is from the conference hall of the original Academy of Sciences, where scientists gathered for discussions.*

ABOVE: *The ground floor boasts fantastic halls of exhibits from each continent, with models wearing authentic costumes.*

OVERLEAF PAGES 28 TO 29: *The Egyptian Bureau, dating from 1825 and designed by F.F. Richter, now the office for African Studies.*

SHEREMETEV PALACE

Boris Petrovich Sheremetev was one of Peter the Great's original Field Marshals. He commanded a force that made Russian history by capturing the fortress dominating the junction of the Neva and Lake Ladoga. For this, he was awarded the title of Count – the first Russian to receive such an honour. After the fortress lost any military significance it became the dreaded Schlüsselburg; prisoners left the Neva Gate of the Peter & Paul Fortress at dawn, to meet their death on the gallows there.

In 1712, Count Sheremetev built a one-storey wooden house on his estate by the Fontanka River, which was later extended by his two sons. The second son, Count Pyotr Borisovich, was the more flamboyant of the two. In 1743 he married a wealthy heiress, a lady-in-waiting to Empress Elizabeth. The new Countess brought a vast fortune to a husband who already owned sixty thousand serfs. Count Pyotr commissioned Savva Chevakinsky to design a new palace, called Fontanny Dom after the river on which it stood. The building is in Baroque style, with white stucco ornamentation on a yellow background and the family crest – a pair of lions holding palm branches – on the central pediment of the portico. Overseeing the work was a talented young serf, Feodor Argunov, who had been sent away while still a child to train as an architect. Another exalted serf was Pearl, a captivating actress from the family's Moscow estate, who won the heart of Count Pyotr's son, Nikolai. They married in 1801, after a long romance during which private theatres were built in all the Sheremetev palaces, including those on the beautiful estates of Kuskova and Ostankino in Moscow.

The Sheremetevs were amongst the wealthiest Russian families, so in Fontanny Dom the rooms were endlessly redecorated; Starov, Quarenghi and Voronikhin are all thought to have worked on the interior. One unusual interior was the ballroom, painted white with a moulded ceiling and a projecting cornice like a narrow gallery all round the room, from which hung groups of close-set candles encircled with crystal drops.

In the mid-19th century, the house was filled with fashionable artists – Glinka was a friend of the family; Pushkin had his portrait painted by Kiprensky, who had a resident studio. In 1837 the building was altered by G.D. Corsini, who also designed the impressive cast-iron railings and grand gates facing the Fontanka, which make the entrance so memorable.

ABOVE: *At long last the interior of the main palace is being restored to its former beauty, having been much divided in the Soviet period when it was the Institute of Arctic Exploration, the largest scientific research centre of its kind in the world. A few rooms have recently been opened to the public as part of the Museum for Musical Instruments.*

LEFT: *The ornate Main Staircase. Many members of the Sheremetev family continued to live in the Palace up until the Revolution.*

BELOW: *Detail of the door in the Etruscan Study. The decoration was based on an Etruscan vase that had just been found during an archaeological dig in Southern Italy.*

In 1867 N.L. Benois added courtyard buildings in the Baroque style. Anna Akhmatova lived here from 1924 to 1952 with Nikolai Punin, an art historian from the Russian Museum. In 1989 their apartment became a museum commemorating the poet. The palace was immortalized in Akhmatova's *Poem Without A Hero*, which describes the ghostly silhouette of the actress, Pearl, shimmering in the White Hall. I now live on the top floor of the converted stables, looking out over the green roof of the palace onto the rippling Fontanka.

RIGHT: *The Raspberry Reception Room with furniture that is stored for the Writer's House, which burnt down in 1989. The wall covering is the original silk, but when the house was used as scientific offices little of the original furniture was kept.*

BOTANICAL GARDENS

The original botanical garden was an open field for growing herbs, begun by Peter the Great to grow medicinal plants brought from Europe. The workers and builders of his new city were falling ill, unused to the marshy climate, badly fed and living in overcrowded conditions. One hundred years later, after a state visit to England, Alexander I decided to open a botanical garden to compete with Kew Gardens and in 1824 the Imperial Botanical Gardens and Library were opened. The gardens cover 16 hectares, with plants from Mexico, South America, Africa, the Far East, and the Caribbean, collected over the years by botanists and travellers.

Before the Revolution, the gardens were the second most

famous in the world, after Kew. Unfortunately the area has been bombed several times – first in 1907, when Stolypin's dacha next door was attacked in an assassination attempt, then in the Second World War. The headquarters of Admiral Tributs were nearby, and Nazi bombs smashed all the glasshouses ruining hundreds of years' worth of plants. Most plants are therefore post–war, and the Botanical Institute, which since the 1830s has been part of the Academy of Sciences, tries to create international exchanges of plants. Currently the gardens have 7,000 types of plant, including giant lilies and lotus flowers. On hot nights in June people flock to see the Tsaritsa

LEFT: *Ornate wrought ironwork from the 19th century.*

BELOW: *One of the 26 working greenhouses, with a collection of 50-year-old Mexican cacti.*

OPPOSITE PAGE:
The Medicinal Orangery was designed in 1888-9 by Nikolai Smirnov and V.P. Samokhvalov. In 1936, it was transferred from the Tauride area to the Botanical gardens and reassembled with its 'popper' style clips. In the foreground is the wild flower garden.

OPPOSITE PAGE: *The Palm Orangery was originally built in 1846-8 by Egor Fisher-Uralsky. It was redesigned 50 years later as the Palm Complex, by Geronimo Kitner, an expert in winter gardens, together with Count Nikolai de Rochefort. Bullet holes can still be seen in the high wrought iron balcony.*

RIGHT: *The raised pond, with giant lilies and lotus flowers. Every colour of lily has a different smell. Visits can be made all year round, and it can be disconcerting to find oneself in a tropical climate with snow on the roof above.*

of the Night, a famous cactus that flowers once a year. There is also a Princess of the Night and some peyote cactus – treasures hidden amongst the greenery.

The Botanical Gardens today have 26 working orangeries/hothouses, covering one hectare of land. The Library contains the original volumes of water-colours, made in 1825 by botanical artist Mattheus; every exhibit in the gardens and orangeries was painted. It also has 18 of the original 200 water-colours bought by Peter the Great, painted on parchment in 1716 by Maria Sybilla Merian, a Dutch botanist who travelled to Mauritania and South America.

The greenhouses are green oases of calm and beauty, recreating the atmosphere of far-away countries close to the city centre. There has been little modernization since the rebuilding after the war; the heating system is old, and the few

LEFT: *The staircase in the Botanical Museum, showing the collection of varieties of wood from around the world. The Museum was built in place of one of the original glasshouses.*

new doors installed in the last few years have warped and no longer open. During their first year, workers walk about like zombies, exhausted by all the fresh air and the plants taking the oxygen. This also happened to me, and I slept as though in a coma for 14 hours after my visit.

ORANIENBAUM

uilt for Alexander Menshikov, Oranienbaum is a large summer palace facing the Gulf of Finland with an estate encompassing forests, two lakes and several smaller palaces and pavilions. The original design for the Grand Palace was by Giovanni Mario Fontana, but Gottfried Schädel began the construction in 1713. He added two curved wings culminating in the Church on the western side

and the Japanese Pavilion, for dances and receptions, on the east. Menshikov, whose princely crown still tops the central roof, was in competition with Peter the Great to build the first summer palace, but the expense bankrupted him and the building was confiscated by the Crown.

In 1743 Oranienbaum was presented by Empress Elizabeth to her nephew Peter. Here, as the reigning Duke of Holstein,

LEFT: *One of the recently reopened rooms in the central section of the Grand Palace. A table is laid with an original tea service; chairs seem to be waiting for the family that once filled these rooms with love.*

OPPOSITE PAGE LEFT: *A carved relief of Catherine, daughter of Grand Duke Michael. She was grandmother to my grandmother, Katya, and adored her first grandchild, bringing her out proudly at grand receptions and treating her as her own child. My grandmother's first conscious memory was being told to wave 'goodbye' as the Grand Duchess's funeral procession passed the Michael Palace, their town residence.*

he played with his Prussian troops, drilling his soldiers and planning the construction of fortresses. It was at this palace that he was forced to abdicate in 1762, which brought his wife, Catherine the Great, to the throne. Immediately after this midsummer coup, despite the unhappy memories of seventeen years of married life, Catherine commissioned Antonio Rinaldi to build the Chinese Palace and the Switchback Pavilion in the grounds. She rarely came to Oranienbaum and it became one of the secondary royal palaces, later passed on to Grand Duke Michael, youngest son of Paul I. It is through Michael's only surviving daughter, Catherine, and her marriage to the first Duke George of Mecklenburg-Strelitz, that the estate came into my grandmother's family.

Their son, also Duke George Mecklenburg-Strelitz, was my great-grandfather and my grandmother was born at Oranienbaum. Now I live in St Petersburg, what fascinates many people is the fact that my family once owned such large properties that were confiscated by the State. How do I feel about this? Am I making claims to get them back? Having been brought up far away in England, I am very logical about my family's lost inheritance. First and foremost, I am the youngest daughter of a second son – and my grandmother had a brother – so I would only have inherited anything in very extreme circumstances. Secondly, Oranienbaum is so large and in such a state of disrepair that my family would also need all the wealth that was stolen in order even to hope to restore it.

Of course I look at the decaying palace with a sense of wistfulness, sometimes imagining what may have been if only... But I also know that in the early 20th century Russia could not have continued without some sort of change. The gap between rich and poor was so vast, the feeling of unrest so vivid. Even my own family lived in a blanketed world of privilege, which could have been misconstrued as stupidity. Yet I have great pride in my roots and very much regret never having met my grandmother and namesake, Katya.

I also believe that bearing the historical name of Galitzine entails a certain amount of responsibility and that the title of 'Princess' – which after all is only a courtesy title nowadays – brings privileges that should be accepted with grace. At the end of the 20th century, now that so many titles are bought or abused, it is far more satisfying to be recognized for personal achievements rather than birthright.

LEFT: *The airy ballroom of the Japanese Pavilion, in the West Wing of the Grand Palace. This wing has been restored in the last five years, since it was vacated by the Soviet naval base that has inhabited the building since the Second World War. Already the foundations are unstable and the East Wing, where the former church stood, is visibly crumbling. The interior of this grand reception room gives the deceptive appearance that all is fine, but the palace is in urgent need of funding if it is to survive.*

ANICHKOV PALACE

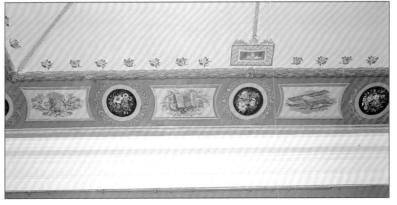

One of the landmarks of Nevsky Prospekt is the Anichkov Bridge over the Fontanka, with its four rearing horses sculpted by Peter Klodt in the 1850s. The Fontanka represented the border of early 19th-century St Petersburg, so the two horses facing the Admiralty are tamed and groomed, while the two facing out are wild and untrained. The bridge takes its name from the Anichkov Palace, which stands on the site of the encampment of Colonel Anichkov, Peter the Great's military engineer.

The original palace was built for Empress Elizabeth's lover,

Alexei Razumovsky – making it one of the earliest in the city. Zemtsov laid the foundations in 1741, but after his death his apprentice G. Dmitriev completed its construction. Nevsky Prospekt was not then the main thoroughfare, so the main façade faced the Fontanka where there was a small dock. In 1776, Catherine the Great presented the Anichkov to her favourite, Grigory Potemkin, who promptly sold it to a merchant to pay off his debts. Patiently, Catherine re-purchased the palace and gave it back to him. In 1778, Starov added a third floor. During the reign of Alexander I, Quarenghi built the white colonnaded building between the main palace and the river, as an arcade for the sale of products from Imperial factories. It later became offices of the Imperial Chancellery, known as the Kabinet. Around this time, the palace was given to the Tsar's sister who employed Rusca to decorate many of the interiors, but little of his work remains due to a fire in 1812. The palace returned to the Crown, and after 1816 Rossi built the service wing, the railings around the diminished garden and two Classical pavilions – one of which now houses a luxurious Versace salon.

Nicholas I lived here before he became Tsar, and in 1826 by Royal order, the palace became the second Imperial palace in the city. Alexander III continued to live at the Anichkov even after his accession; he found the Winter Palace cold and empty and used it only for formal functions. On the announcement of their engagement, my own grandparents were presented to the Dowager Empress Maria Feodorovna here. At the beginning of February 1914, Maria Feodorovna gave a great ball at the Anichkov to introduce her two eldest grand-daughters, Olga and Tatyana, into society. It was the last fashionable function at which she was seen but she continued to live in the palace until she abandoned St Petersburg in 1916.

After the Bolshevik take-over of 1917, the Anichkov Palace was one of many Museums of the City, showing the looted wealth of the aristocracy. Most of the palace was reconstructed in 1935 by architects Gegello and Krichevsky to make a Palace for Pioneers – the grandest one in the country. They created halls and a 300-seat cinema on the third floor. The Pioneer organization was founded in 1922, part of the Young Communists' League for children between eight and 14 years old. Little Pioneers clad in blue uniforms with red cravats marched around the Soviet Union, displaying patriotism and shouting that they were 'Always Ready!' to serve the state. This palace has thus seen much of St Petersburg's history, from mazurkas at Romanov receptions to the patter of excited children's feet at Party pageants.

RIGHT: *Alexander III's study: 'When he lived here the imperial palace became just what it should be – a place housing the busiest man in Russia.' Grand Duke Alexander Mikhailovich in his memoirs.*

OPPOSITE PAGE TOP: *When the palace was reconstructed as a Palace for Pioneers, two rooms for telling Russian folk tales were decorated with illustrations from stories by Pushkin and Gorky in the Palekh style.*

OPPOSITE PAGE BOTTOM: *Soviet plafond depicting aeroplanes, sickles and other unexpected 20th-century images.*

ABOVE: *This room was once the study of Dowager Empress Maria Feodorovna, but the original decor, which was designed in 1865 by Ernest Jibert (1823-1909), has not survived.*

OVERLEAF PAGES 40 TO 41: *In the gardens was an ice rink in winter, while flowers and tropical plants bloomed in the winter garden inside, built by Rakhau in 1875. A winter garden is a grand conservatory, a feature of many palaces from the late 19th century. Here, in the depths of the long Russian winter, the hostess could sit amidst greenery and imagine the Spring.*

MINING INSTITUTE

The Ural mountains have existed for over 250 million years and their wealth of minerals is internationally famous. Peter the Great started mining there, bringing in teachers from Europe. It was Catherine the Great, as part of her educational reforms, who set up the First Higher Technical Institute in Russia in 1773 (the second in the world). Originally it occupied six small houses at the end of the Neva Embankment on Vassilievsky Island.

In 1777, King Gustav III of Sweden was the first important guest, and he was so impressed by the mineral collection that he later sent a gift of over 300 precious stones and rubies, which can still be seen today. The collection in the Mineral Cabinets grew, as Tsars and nobles, professors and collectors all donated their own stones. In the 1780s a huge lump of malachite was presented to Catherine by a prospector in the Urals and she added it to the collection. The major pieces on display were either gifts from visiting dignitaries or the best pieces from Russian soil, after Nicholas I decreed that these were to stay in Russia. All gold found in the country at this time had to be sent directly to the capital, to be stored in the Mint.

The Higher Technical Institute later became The Mining Institute, which now occupies a building specially commissioned by Alexander I, part of the panorama seen from the Winter Palace. It was designed by Andrei Voronikhin, who in 1806-11 created one large building out of the six houses, adding a new west wing. Voronikhin was the brilliant serf from Perm, whose artistic talent was spotted by his landowner, Count Stroganov. Voronikhin was sent to Moscow to develop his painting technique, where his talent for architecture was noted by Bazhenov. Thanks to the sponsorship of Stroganov, Voronikhin was then enrolled in the St Petersburg Academy of Arts. After a Grand Tour of Europe with the Count's son, he studied for several years in Paris and Rome and finally returned to Russia to impart his knowledge of the latest European versions of Neo-Classical design and decoration.

It was from the Greek tradition that Voronikhin took his inspiration for the Mining Institute; it is modelled on the Temple of Poseidon at Paestum. The central portico with its 12 columns is a fine example of pure Greek Classicism, with wings set back in order to accentuate the entrance and a thinly drawn pediment against a plain wall. Inside, the only remaining features of Voronikhin's original work are the six-point staircase with its iron balustrade and the clock – no longer working – guarded by two dwarfs. It was his last important building,

ABOVE TOP: *The only remaining features of Voronikhin's original work are the six-point staircase with its iron balustrade and* (ABOVE) *the clock guarded by two dwarfs.*

OPPOSITE PAGE: *The Column Hall was the work of Alexander Ivanovich Postnikov (1766-1830). Its ceiling panel features three allegorical scenes with Peter the Great, Catherine the Great and Alexander I, and was originally created by Giovanni Battista Scotti. The hall was destroyed during the Second World War, but has been carefully restored.*

but the influence of Greek style began a trend in Russian architecture called Alexandrian Classicism, which affected not just the façades of buildings but also their interiors.

The stunning interior of the Column Hall was the work of Alexander Ivanovich Postnikov (1766-1830), while its ceiling panel, with three allegorical scenes featuring Peter the Great, Catherine the Great and Alexander I, was originally created by Giovanni Battista Scotti. Unfortunately the hall was destroyed during the Second World War, so what is now seen is a reconstruction.

The first collection to be bought in its entirety, by Alexander I in the early 1800s, was the Forster Collection. It consisted of over 5,000 objects and cost 50,000 roubles, paid over a period of 10 years with no interest. Included was a large piece of calcite clustered with superb Colombian emeralds but, in 1916, against a background of increasing unrest in Petrograd, there was a robbery at the Mining Institute and the precious rock went missing. The crime had been organized by two workers and eventually the piece of calcite was found, but the emeralds had been reduced in size and quantity.

A pre-Revolutionary catalogue still exists, compiled by the museum's curator, Melnikov, and itemizing each exhibit. The collection has greatly diminished since then – and not solely as a result of the 1916 robbery. When I asked if the Bolsheviks had raided the safes for gold, platinum and diamonds (which had been kept here and were only moved to Moscow in 1920),

LEFT: *One room houses the skeletons of prehistoric animals, along with animal horns and antlers.*

OPPOSITE PAGE: *Display cabinets designed by Meyer for Catherine the Great's mineral collection in the Hermitage. They were moved here in 1816 by Alexander I, who decided to use them to exhibit Russian minerals.*

RIGHT: *An iron palm tree, beaten out from a single railway sleeper. It was originally made for the All Russia Industrial Exhibition of 1896-98 held in Nizhny-Novgorod, which featured many graduates and exhibits from the Mining Institute.*

LEFT: *A huge lump of malachite, weighing over 1500 kg, presented to Catherine in the 1780s by a prospector in the Urals.*

I was told they left the Institute and Museum as it was, because the valuable pieces were heavy and the soldiers respected the miners...

Today, every vitrine and showcase at the Mining Institute is full of examples of thousands of different minerals and precious stones. One of the oldest exhibits is a model of a gold mine, constructed using real minerals, metals and precious stones, given to Catherine in 1776. There is also a small collection of Fabergé items that can only be seen with the permission of the curator, or in touring exhibitions. The Institute not only houses this amazing mineral collection but also the Academy of Mining, which has had many famous graduates – including General Wrangel and Tchaikovsky's father.

RUSSIAN ORTHODOX CHURCH

Whether touched by the purity of unaccompanied singing, or by the opulence of priestly robes, or just the simplicity of candlelight flickering on an icon, it is hard to remain unaffected by the Russian church. The smell of incense, the deep chanting monotone of the priest, the fervent crossing of the congregation – all are ingredients of a faith that has remained unchanged since its arrival in Russia in the 10th century.

The Great Prince Vladimir of Kiev Rus adopted Christianity in its Byzantine form in 988. Trading of 'slaves' was the most important aspect of the Kiev economy, and the rapid conversion of pagan tribes owed much of its success to the close trade relations with Constantinople. The threat of eternal damnation to non-believers also helped the Church to gain authority. The Roman Catholic Church eventually broke away from the Byzantine in 1054, having quarrelled over differences in the Nicene Creed since the 5th century.

The Orthodox Church allows 'no graven image of anything that is in heaven above', as written in the Ten Commandments, hence the development of the icon. These are a holy undertaking; the hand of the artist is guided by the Spirit of God and the colours were once mixed with holy water and particles of the relics of saints. The pictures have no perspective, following graphic rules handed down from generation to generation. Simple icons were hung in every house, while famous icons performed miracles and had cathedrals named after them – the Kazan Mother of God, for example, where General Kutuzov prayed before his victory at the Battle of Borodino (1812).

The church sanctuary is divided from the nave by the iconostasis screen. The central Imperial Gate is used only by the priest (and the Tsar on his coronation), the two side gates are the deacon's gates. Above are icons of the Virgin Mother and the saints, with the central icon representing Jesus Christ. The oldest surviving iconostasis is in the Archangel Cathedral in the Moscow Kremlin, executed by the most famous icon painter of all, Andrei Rublev, at the end of the 14th century.

The history of the Orthodox faith in Russia is eventful. During the reforms of Patriarch Nikon in 1653, the Old Believers split from the established church. In 1721, Peter the Great abolished the Patriarchate and reduced the Church to a government department, the Holy Synod, and in 1797 Paul I declared the Tsar Head of the Church. The last Empress, Alexandra Feodorovna, prayed devoutly and covered her walls with icons, hoping to cure her haemophiliac son.

The Bolsheviks persecuted the Church as a threat to their cause – of 54,000 churches, only a few hundred were left undesecrated. During the Second World War, Stalin, a trained priest, allowed the revival of some churches.

ABOVE: *With the resurgence of believers, small villages are now setting up their own churches. Icons are collected or made, embroidered cloths are given to decorate them for different occasions, the candle holders appear – either someone has managed to save them at home or they are found in antique shops. Generally the congregation is made up of elderly women – for whom the church is the centre of their life, so they are willing to clean and serve it to the best of their ability.*

RIGHT: *The upper iconostasis of the Cathedral of St Nicholas of the Sea, the sailors' church, built by Savva Chevakinsky in 1753. The two-storey cathedral is built in Russian Baroque style, like Rastrelli's Smolny Cathedral, with golden cupolas and a separate bell tower. Many valuable icons have been collected here, including ten icons in gold frames, presented by Catherine the Great to commemorate the victories of the Russian fleet, and some relics from Naples of St Alexander, brought by the Empress Alexandra Feodorovna, wife of Nicholas I.*

BELOW: *In a banned letter to Gogol, the critic Belinsky wrote: 'The Russian says about the icon – "If it does you good pray before it, if not use it as a cover for the cooking pots"'. This attitude was not exceptional among the pre-Revolutionary intelligentsia and was shared by the Bolsheviks, who saw the Orthodox Church as their most formidable enemy.*

Throughout Russian history, the Orthodox clergy preached submission to the State and continued to do so in Soviet times, but believers were not allowed Communist Party membership and services were supervised by the KGB. Since the 1980s there has been a religious revival, with churches rebuilt and congregations spilling onto the streets at the beautiful Easter services. At the end of the 19th century Engels predicted that Russia would never succumb to Communism, because of the Church. The Bolsheviks tried to create an atheist State, but the Orthodox faith was simmering below the surface for 75 years.

OVERLEAF PAGES 48 TO 49: *The chapel at the St Sergius-Trinity, the work of young monks at this recently re-established monastery. Situated on the road to Peterhof, the monastery was founded during the reign of Anna Ivanovna in 1732, and served as a sanctuary to many famous figures throughout St Petersburg's history. The architect Stakenschneider was buried here, as was the first Zinaida Yusupova and other members of wealthy families. In 1919-20, the authorities closed the monastery, arresting and shooting the remaining priests. The premises were taken over by the Police Academy in Soviet times and the monk's chapel was made into a cinema for cadets.*

NAVAL MUSEUM

The Stock Exchange building, which now houses the Naval Museum, is one of the finest edifices in St Petersburg. Built by Thomas de Thomon at the expense of the merchants of the city, it is situated on Vassilievsky Spit at the point where the Neva converges with her smaller tributary, the Nevka.

Peter the Great had encouraged trade in his new capital and established a stock exchange on this same spot, known as the Dutch Exchange, where traders bought and sold their wares in the open air. In 1783, Quarenghi began designing a building to house the Exchange, but due to the Turko-Russian war the work was postponed. The French architect Thomas de Thomon – who prior to his arrival in Russia had built nothing – was invited by Alexander I to complete the project. Like Voronikhin, he used the Classical style of the Greek Temple at Paestum, a basilica set on a granite stylobate supporting 44 Doric columns. Above the eastern colonnade the building rises to a gable, with a large semi-circular window framing a sculptural group of Neptune and Two Rivers by I. Prokofiev.

The Stock Exchange was opened in 1810. Brokers, clerks, merchants and managers all needed a special pass, or stock exchange ticket, to enter. A broker had to meet specific requirements: to be at least 30 years old, a Russian subject and either a merchant of the 1st or 2nd Guilds or a Guild manager. Unofficial brokers did exist, but they risked being caught by the Court Broker, an official assigned by the Minister of Finance, who was responsible for supervising brokers' activities and the determination of quotations. Vessels could moor at the quays, and warehouses were built along the Nevka embankment to store cargo.

After the Bolshevik Revolution commercial trading stopped and the building became redundant until 1940, when the Central Naval Museum moved in. Unfortunately, the lead used to seal round the 19th-century base was later taken to make bullets during the Siege, and this has caused structural problems in the foundations. In spring, when the ice melts, water pours into the basement rooms that are used as museum

ABOVE: *The Classical staircase now features warheads and statues of naval heroes. The Naval Museum was founded by Peter the Great in 1709, and was first based in the Admiralty. Some of the original exhibits can still be seen today, such as the famous hollowed out log known as 'Botik', the boat in which Peter learnt to sail as a boy. This simple wooden vessel inspired his love of sailing and hence has been dubbed 'The Grandfather of the Russian Fleet'.*

storage space. The surrounding pediment therefore remains out of bounds to the public, although the flimsy barriers were removed during the State visit of HM Queen Elizabeth in 1994. There are now plans for the Naval Museum to be moved to the Admiralty, so that the Stock Exchange can be re-established in its original location.

ACADEMY OF ARTS

The cold northern light filters through dusty studio windows onto naked models in Classical poses, draped in velvet and bearing fruit; another life-drawing class begins at the Academy of Arts. Not much has changed since 1764, when the Imperial Academy of Fine Arts was opened by order of Catherine the Great. Her purpose was to create an official form of art, rather than develop the individuality of the students: 'Art must aim at revealing virtue, at immortalizing the deeds of the great men who deserve the nation's gratitude and at encouraging the heart and mind to emulate them with these historical paintings.'

In Catherine's time the course lasted fifteen years, now it is six. Competition is very fierce, attracting students from all over the former Soviet Union to fill the 15 places for painting, 10 for architecture and 10 for sculpture. The Classical technique is taught during the first year in most art schools, but at the Academy Classical training goes on for the full six years – it is one of the few places left in the world where a rigorous training of this kind can be found. Originality is only allowed to surface if it follows Classical rules. In this art school, there is just one way of portraying things and no freedom of expression, so the students' work tends to look very similar. Drawings are torn up or defaced if not accurate.

The strict symmetry of the Academy building, begun in 1764 by Jean-Baptiste Vallin de la Mothe, mirrors the style of teaching. The huge building stands alone on the bank of the Neva, guarded by two sphinxes, which – as legend has it – miraculously appeared out of the sea in 1832. Long corridors and classrooms surround a perfectly circular courtyard; the words 'Architecture', 'Sculpture', 'Drawing' and 'Engraving', the four Classical crafts, decorate the four porticoes.

The first floor contains a permanent exhibition of graduates' work, beginning in Catherine's time and moving chronologically through Classicism to Social Realism. It includes the diploma works of famous graduates of the Academy, such as Repin (after whom the Academy was renamed in 1944) Serov, Vrubel, Bakst, Lanceray, the architect Fomin and Nicholas II's

favourite artist, Kuinghi. It also features the work of my own teacher of sculpture, Mikhail Anikushin, who later became Head of the Sculpture department. On the third floor are exquisite architectural maquettes, miniature versions of masterpieces in the city, including Rastrelli's project for St Nicholas Cathedral, examples of town planning by Rossi, the Classical works of Thomas de Thomon, Vallin de la Mothe,

Quarenghi and Montferrand and various proposals for St Isaac's.

The Academy now has a History of Art course and foreign paying students, allowing outside influences in; it was only after the 1991 coup that lectures about Lenin's influence on Soviet art were dropped. The facilities remain old-fashioned, however, due to dependence on government funding, and professors are strict to the point of pedantry. Students work slowly, with little knowledge of the commercial side of art, but with a pure belief that the arts offer a higher spirituality. This was all very well when government grants covered subsidized housing, materials and food, but with the new market economy in Russia, most former graduates have been left in unrealistic financial situations. They are able to execute perfect paintings, but in a style that has little market value today. Many of the portrait painters under the arches of Nevsky Prospekt are Academy graduates, while many bronze and china souvenirs are the work of sculptors trained at the Academy.

Also within the building is the recently restored Church of St Catherine, built in the 1820s and named after the Academy's founder. In Soviet times it was the social club.

OPPOSITE PAGE TOP:
The atelier of Taras Shevchenko, recreated in 1964 on the 150th anniversary of his birth and opened as a museum. The room is an attractive example of a 19th-century artist's studio, with atmosphere and charm.

OPPOSITE PAGE BOTTOM:
The plasterwork department makes some of the casts used in the restoration of palaces.

ABOVE: *The sculpture gallery on the ground floor contains plaster casts from Egyptian times through to French Classicism, allowing students to pass through all the masterpieces of the civilized world in one circuit.*

LEFT: *One of the four libraries. The shelves hold priceless volumes and etchings dating back to Catherine the Great's collection.*

OVERLEAF PAGE 54:
Main staircase showing the Classical influence that pervades the building.

THE AGE OF EMPIRE

THIS WAS A TIME OF WAR AND PEACE, balls at Court, men in uniform, secret societies and duels. A multi-faceted and brilliant Court society was developing in a vast and formidable empire. St Petersburg underwent the most grandiose town planning initiative so far, with many a Classical ensemble being created; the most noticeable was the yellow and white ordered beauty created by the Italian architect, Carlo Rossi. A visitor to St Petersburg today essentially sees the façade of this 19th century Tsarist city, a multitude of spires and columns divided by the weather-beaten Neva, under the wide northern sky.

The Court of Alexander I was dominated by the Dowager Empress Maria Feodorovna, and lived in sublime indifference to the concerns of ordinary people. Education was still limited to a tiny elite. The 'angel' Tsar began his reign intending to introduce a constitutional monarchy, but as he became more haunted by the murder of his father, Paul I, and disillusioned by French Enlightenment, he became more religious and repressive.

The 19th century began with an epoch-making event: the Patriotic War of 1812. As a result of this war there was a surge of patriotism, which gave a tremendous boost to the folk theme in fine arts and meant that people concentrated more on Russian sources. Officers returning from Paris ordered Empire furniture in Russian materials, such as Karelian birch and malachite, and the period of Alexandrine Classicism was born.

PAVILIONS

When visiting the palaces near St Petersburg, a walk in the park can suddenly reveal an unexpected delight – a magical pavilion, built by one of the great architects on a royal whim. At Peterhof and the Catherine Palace only engravings remain to show what stood before, but at Oranienbaum, Gatchina and Pavlovsk three treasures lie hidden in the trees.

It was Catherine the Great who developed the estate of Oranienbaum between 1762 and 1774, when she commissioned Antonio Rinaldi to build the Chinese Palace and Katalnaya Gorka (Switchback Pavilion), which resembles a heavily-iced wedding cake the colour of the Summer sky. The pavilion

BELOW: *Duke George of Mecklenburg-Strelitz had one of the finest collections of Meissen figurines, some of which are still on display in the Porcelain Room of Katalnaya Gorka.*

originally had a wooden roller coaster to one side, and was built purely to give shelter to members of the court who were amusing themselves on 'la montaigne Russe'. Usually sledging was a winter pastime, for which ice-hills were constructed in public spaces; Katalnaya Gorka was built to enable this pastime to continue during the summer months. The roller coaster was surrounded by an open colonnade with a flat roof for spectators. Inside the pavilion, privileged guests could relax after all the fresh air and excitement, regaining composure before venturing outside again.

The Birch Pavilion at Gatchina was an entirely secret construction, a wife's romantic gift to her beloved husband. Hidden amidst the trees is a huge pile of birch logs, but when a camouflaged door opens the log-pile reveals its true identity. The lightness, the secrecy, the opulence were all the fantasy of sweet Maria Feodorovna, who saw a similar log cabin in France in 1781 and invited Nikolai Lvov to design one for her melancholic husband, Paul. Still not Tsar, living in the shadow of his domineering mother and haunted by the murder of his father, Paul suffered long bouts of depression, only relieved by

ABOVE: *'The Rose Pavilion consists of 3 or 4 small rooms and a large hall, which was added when the Emperor returned from the war. It is still hung with garlands of roses and laurels, which the Institutes made for the feast the Dowager Empress gave for her son... We supped at little tables, and at 10 o'clock carriages drove us home.' Diary of Cornelie de Wassnaer, 1825.*

ABOVE: *The garlands of silk roses were sewn by hand.*

OPPOSITE PAGE: *Model of Katalnya Gorka from drawings by Rinaldi, showing the original switchback. Special carriages were designed by Andrei Nartov to roll down the wooden coasting path, which stretched for 532m. The roller coaster became hazardous in the late 19th century and was dismantled.*

the endless drilling of soldiers. The original pavilion was razed to the ground during the Second World War, but has been restored and once more manages to capture some of the romance intended by Paul's long-suffering wife.

Maria Feodorovna was also responsible for another charming building: the Rose Pavilion at Pavlovsk. In 1814, when it was built, she was Dowager Empress and mother to Tsar Alexander I. Thrilled at her son's triumphant return from Paris, she planned a grand party for the Russian Guard in the Rose Pavilion. The task of adding and decorating a ballroom fell to Carlo Rossi, personally supervised by Maria Feodorovna who arranged the festivities down to the last detail. Roses decorated the ceiling, the walls and the arches, and chains of hand-sewn silk roses hung in graceful loops from the central chandelier. Aeolian harps were built into the window frames, to sing in the rose-scented breeze from the surrounding garden. In summer 1997 the rose bushes were replaced and the Rose Pavilion reopened, after a generous donation from Veuve Cliquot, who supplied the champagne that flowed at the first Victory Ball.

ABOVE: *Inside the Birch Pavilion is a delicate salon with mirrored walls framed in floral trellis work.*

RIGHT: *At Gatchina, the huge pile of birch logs set amongst the trees initially gives the impression that the woodsman has been very busy. On closer inspection, the log-pile is revealed to be the ingenious Birch Pavilion – designed as a surprise for Paul I.*

STONE ISLAND PALACE

Stone Island (Kamenny Ostrov) is one of the islands of the Neva Delta. It was first owned by Count Bestuzhev-Ryumin, Chancellor to Empress Elizabeth, who brought thousands of serfs from the Ukraine to improve his estate. In 1765, Catherine the Great bought the island, along with Bestuzhev's wooden villa, for her son Paul, but as he was only eight years old construction of his Palace did not begin until Spring of 1776.

No one is exactly sure which architect was responsible for Stone Island Palace but it is believed that the design was by Vassily Bazhenov. After Catherine dropped him, the palace was most probably built by Yuri Velten, with interiors by Stasov. A well-proportioned, two-storey building in yellow and white stucco, with a courtyard leading to the informal

English garden by Thomas de Thomon, it is one of the earliest examples in Russia of Neo-classicism, a style which carried on for over half a century.

Abandoned by Paul and Maria Feodorovna who preferred Pavlovsk, the palace was used by the deposed king of Poland, Stanislaw Poniatowski – often thought to be Paul's father. Later it became the favourite summer residence of Alexander I. On August 8, 1812, it was the scene of a historic meeting between the Emperor and Prince Kutuzov, at which plans were made for the war against Napoleon. After the death of Alexander, the island passed to his youngest brother, Grand Duke Michael, whose descendants owned it until the Revolution, when it became 'Workers' Island'.

Throughout the Soviet Union the large palaces of the rich were converted into sanatoriums. These were a cross between a hotel, a health spa and an institution; they were fully staffed with cooks, cleaners, administrators and gardeners, as well as medical staff, masseurs and dieticians. The idea was to provide supervised holidays, within a supervised environment – a kind of government package tour.

Only privileged workers or those with health problems could come to a sanatorium. Each Union had its own: the Union of Artists had one in the Vatican, the Union of Botanists owns Nikitinsky Gardens near Yalta and factories – such as the Kirov Factory – also laid claim to various establishments. The sanatorium on Stone Island has psychiatrists to rehabilitate military pilots, and is of a high standard. Patients can take mud baths, be hosed down with salty water, walk in the park, take excursions to museums, eat balanced meals and sleep – the most popular form of relaxation for Russians. There is also space for the family – although often time spent in a sanatorium was a break from home life too.

Now there is no funding coming from the State, these places are looking for other ways of generating income such as becoming private boarding schools or health clubs. As the West becomes more comprehensive, Russia becomes more exclusive.

RIGHT: *The spartan metal beds with equipment from the 1950s look very incongruous against the Classical trimmings of the palace. Rooms have been divided into dormitories and sections for various treatments, such as UV light, massage and physiotherapy.*

The Deux Français, who visited the palace in 1791-2 managed to snoop about, even into grand-ducal bedrooms. They wrote of the palace: 'It is extremely pretty, especially on account of the site; one goes up a few steps to the ground floor, and finds first a fairly big antechamber, with arabesques, then a salon of oval shape, whose length makes it look rather narrow; the decoration is very simple. At the right a room with a communicating door into a charming little theatre. The bedroom of their Highnesses is very prettily furnished; there is a very beautiful mantel of marble and porphyry: on a table, a marble bust of the Grand Duchess, which is an excellent likeness… The façade on the garden is ornamented with columns… at the end of the garden there is a little brick chapel; the gothic style which they have tried to imitate, makes a pretty effect.'

RUSSIAN NATIONAL LIBRARY

Catherine the Great ordered her ambassadors throughout Europe to keep her informed of interesting sales in the Arts. In 1765, her Ambassador in Paris, Prince Dmitry Galitzine (also responsible for purchasing many paintings for Catherine's Hermitage) learned that Diderot was planning to sell the library he had amassed for his work on the *Encyclopaedié*. The Empress offered more money than he was asking, and appointed him librarian of his own books. After including his own manuscripts in the sale, Diderot received outright the equivalent of his salary for 50 years. From having had money difficulties, he suddenly found himself with a fortune of 41,000 livres. The Diderot library came to Russia and became the Imperial Library.

The first Library building was built on the corner of Nevsky Prospekt and Ulitsa Sadovaya by Yegor Sokolov in 1796–1801. In 1828-32, Rossi created the principal façade facing Alexandra Garden, which is adorned with 18 Ionic columns and statues of Greek philosophers, as part of the ensemble around the Alexandrinsky Theatre. A statue of Minerva, the goddess of wisdom, crowns the building, and on her helmet is the smallest sphinx in St Petersburg, the work of sculptor V. Demut-Malinovsky. These Classical references are meant to represent the enormous wealth of knowledge stored within the building's walls.

In 1814, the first reading room was opened, seating just 46 people. By this time the Imperial Public Library held 238,000 volumes. This formed the basis of what is now The Russian National Library, with stocks of over 20 million books – together with maps, manuscripts, photographs and documents, over 32 million items – making it the second largest library in Russia, (the Lenin Library in Moscow being the largest). Some of the rarities in the collection include: 7,000 volumes of Voltaire's personal library, the first book ever printed in Russian dating from 1564, the first Russian newspaper dating from 1703, Dostoevsky's diary for 1880, and the smallest printed book in the world – a version of Krylov's fables the size of a postage stamp. One of the most valuable collections of 15th-century incunabula in the world is kept in the Gothic 'Cabinet of Faust', a copy of a monastic library designed in 1857 by architect I.I. Gornostaev. There are also other curious items such as police reports on Voltaire (which were thrown out of the Bastille during the French Revolution and picked up by Vladimir Dubrovsky, the Russian Ambassador in Paris), the prayer book of Mary, Queen of Scots, which she

supposedly took to the scaffold, and a collection of autographs including signatures of Peter the Great, Marie Antoinette, General Suvorov, Robespierre and Byron.

During the Second World War the semi-circular building

LEFT & BELOW LEFT: *The Alexander I room, now used to store over 200,000 rare manuscripts. The oldest dated Russian manuscript is the Ostromir Gospel (1056), while the first printed Russian book is The Acts of the Apostles (Moscow 1564). Some manuscripts date back to 3AD. Special vitrines exhibit Oriental manuscripts and parchments, but some extremely rare pieces – such as the 9th Century Qu'ran of Caliph Osman in Kufic characters – were returned to the Moslem peoples of the Soviet Union after the Revolution. In the original room was a register for readers to sign, the first signature is that of Tsar Alexander I.*

OPPOSITE PAGE: *The Reading Room for Medical Technology, designed in 1896 by Yevgrat Vorotilov, seats 500 readers. This reading room had to be closed during the Second World War, as it was in the line of fire.*

was shelled continuously, but thankfully the majority of the collection, including the rare books and manuscripts, had been sent to Ulyanovsk for safety. The iron shutters in the Oval Room, once the room of Alexander I, have remained closed due to damage from enemy bullets. During the Siege of Leningrad readers still came to use the Library, although they were fainting with hunger and there was no heating or electricity. In fact, those who kept up an interest in something survived the Blockade better than those who stayed in bed.

A year after Peter the Great's death there were just seven books published in the whole of the Russian Empire; some 250 years later, Russia is one of the most literary and literate nations in the world.

RIGHT: *Built in 1857 in the style of a monastic library, the Cabinet of Faust is the special reading room for incunabula. The Library holds over 6,000 volumes, one of the most valuable collections in the world. Open on the table is* Lancelot du Lac, *c.1500, with its illuminated illustrations – this volume alone is worth $3million.*

BELOW: *There are five reading rooms in the Russian National Library, this is the one for Art and Literature. Despite it being the public library, familiarly known as 'Publichka', every reader has to have a reader's ticket before being allowed in. To obtain such a ticket, you must either have completed higher education, or have a letter of reference to show you are studying or researching.*

PRIYUTINO

Just outside St Petersburg there is a marvellous 19th-century sanctuary called Priyutino. The name means shelter or refuge, and it was once the dacha, or summer home, of Alexei Nikolaevich Olenin (1764-1843). Olenin was an archaeologist, writer, sponsor of the arts, first Director of the Imperial St Petersburg Public Library and the Head of the Academy of Arts, and a popular friend of many of the important cultural figures of the time. He was the man responsible for commissioning the Alexander Column, built in Palace Square in memory of Russia's victory over Napoleon in 1812.

The land on which Priyutino stands was bought in 1795 with the dowry of Olenin's wife, Elizabeth Markovna. The property is a simple red brick two-storey house, with a separate kitchen and servants' quarters built in the same style. There are various out-houses including a blacksmith's foundry and a dairy built like a Roman pantheon. The lower storeys

RIGHT: *Main salon, recreated exactly as it was in the time of the Olenin family, based on a watercolour by Feodor Sonzev painted on 26 May 1834. His painting even included the guests of that day.*

OPPOSITE PAGE: *Priyutino is a shrine to Empire Classicism at its peak. The house has a magical atmosphere because the present day curators love the place almost as much as the past owners.*

BELOW: *The curators have painstakingly collected and restored Empire furniture, and recreated the style of 200 years ago when the house was filled with prominent guests.*

of each of these are in unworked stone; because of this, it is thought that the architect Nikolai Alexandrovich Lvov had something to do with the design – he certainly knew Olenin through the Academy of Arts.

The house always remained Elizabeth's and she brought a homely, comforting atmosphere to the place. Guests were free to wander about and amuse themselves as they chose; everything was very informal apart from mealtimes, to which guests were summoned by the ringing of a bell. When the guests were not eating, there was much romancing and philosophizing. Cards were rarely played – the most lively pastime was considered to be interesting conversation and discussions on Classical art, history and the arts of Ancient Russia. Glinka sometimes performed his romances and even Griboedev played the piano. Krylov, renowned for his Russian versions of Aesop's fables, was an enthusiastic player of charades. He was such a regular guest that he was almost a member of the family, with his own room above the banya where he created his stories. The atmosphere was obviously conducive to writing, as Pushkin, Griboedev and Gnedich (the Russian poet who translated Homer's *Iliad*) all produced memorable works whilst staying at Priyutino. Some of Pushkin's most lyrical verses on love were composed whilst enamoured of Anna Olenina, the younger

daughter of the house. He wrote the poem on the right in her album.

The park surrounding the house is a gentle and romantic place, with a lake surrounded by trees. There is a marble sundial in the grounds and nearby once stood a mausoleum to Olenin's eldest son, Nikolai, who was killed at Borodino.

After Elizabeth's death in 1838 the estate was sold, as it seemed empty and cold without her presence. Since the Olenin family moved on, the estate has had several private owners, the last of whom emigrated to Germany, but none of these added such colour to its story. When all land was taken over by the

I loved you: and perhaps that love
still burns within my soul today;
But do not let it trouble you;
I would not sadden you in any way.
Silently, hopelessly I loved you,
Sometimes jealous, sometimes too shy;
May God grant you be loved by another,
As sincerely and as tenderly as I.

ALEXANDER PUSHKIN

State the house became a dairy. During the Second World War, Priyutino was an hospital for wounded pilots. The 'Road of Life' passed its gates; this was the route used by women bringing bread into the city from Lake Ladoga during the 900-day Siege of Leningrad. After the war the various buildings on the estate were converted to communal living, but the residents all moved out in the 1970s.

Priyutino is now a shrine to Empire Classicism at its peak. The house has a magical atmosphere because the present day curators love the place almost as much as the past owners. They have painstakingly collected and restored furniture of the

OPPOSITE PAGE: *Desk in the corner of Olenin's study, with busts showing his love of Classical art.*

ABOVE: *Elizabeth Markovna's bedroom has a feminine decor. The house remained hers, and she brought a homely, comforting atmosphere to the place.*

period, and recreated the style of 200 years ago when the house was filled with prominent guests. The storerooms are full of old Russian clothes, costumes and uniforms. Until recently, foreigners on tour buses were not allowed to visit because the access route passed near to the Polygon, a military test site. Now the laws have changed, and once again the house is filled with a variety of visitors.

MONTFERRAND

LEFT & ABOVE: *The main hall of Montferrand's private house, decorated by his assistant V.A. Shreiber in 1845-6. Some of the outstanding plasterwork remains, together with the original Venetian fireplace.*

St Petersburg has been built by many talented architects, but probably the most extraordinary was August Montferrand. Born in France in 1786, he studied architecture in Paris but worked in St Petersburg after 1816. His greatest works are landmarks of the city: St Isaac's Cathedral and the Alexander Column. Both were built in celebration of Russia's victory over Napoleon.

Tsar Alexander I set up a competition to rebuild the cathedral dedicated to the patron saint of Peter the Great, who was born on May 30, the feast day of St Isaac of Dalmatia. Montferrand submitted a beautifully bound album with 24 different schemes – there were designs in Chinese, Indian, Gothic and Byzantine styles. He was an inexperienced architect but a very good draughtsman, and his presentation so impressed the Tsar that he was chosen as Court architect. It was two years before building work could commence because there were so many inaccuracies in his plans. Even the construction work was halted several times owing to mistakes in the final design.

Built over a period of 40 years (1818-58), the ultimate result was one of the last great Neo-classical buildings in Europe and the most incongruous, yet dramatic, focal point of the city. It is the fourth church on the site: the first was a small wooden St Isaac's, built in 1710 near the Admiralty; a small stone version by Rinaldi was begun in 1768, but as it neared completion under Brenna in 1802 it was considered too small, so a third and larger building was begun immediately.

In the story of St Isaac, he miraculously drags himself out of a swamp into which he had been thrown by Emperor Valens. This could be seen as a parallel to the building of the Cathedral, which needed foundations of thousands of timber piles, as deep as the 48 monolithic columns of granite are high, to allow the structure to stand firm on the capital's swampy soil. To transport the 114-ton columns into position special ships and tackle were needed, and a small railway had to be built. The dome was constructed over iron ribs, with craftsmen working to their death as they inhaled mercury fumes while gilding the

RIGHT: *The bronze staircase behind the entrance to the house, which is through a tiny door from the first courtyard. The building now houses industrial offices, so the frescoes that decorated the walls have been covered over with several layers of thick gloss paint.*

RIGHT: *Wonderful contrasts can be found in the house: electric digital clocks inlaid into ornate mantelpieces, the hammer and sickle carefully modelled and gilded, surrounded by a golden garland.*

FAR RIGHT: *St Isaac's has the third largest dome in Europe – the cupola is 800sqm, with a painting of the Virgin by Bryullov. A popular superstition existed that the Romanov dynasty would end on completion of St Isaac's, which may also account for the length of the building process. Montferrand's image can be seen in cast iron on the west portico.*

exterior. The structure was complete by 1842, but it took until May 1858 – one month before Montferrand's death – to decorate the interior. No expense was spared: frescoes, mosaics and relief work decorated the walls and 43 different types of stone and marble were used in the ornamentation, with pillars of jasper, malachite and lapis-lazuli.

During the building of St Isaac's, Montferrand lived in a small two-storey house on the Moika. The interior was decorated at the same time as the Cathedral's interior, by his assistant Vladimir A. Shreiber. Montferrand divided the courtyard into two sections: the inner half had a small landscape garden and the outer displayed his private collection of antique sculptures. Before his death, Montferrand asked Alexander II for permission to be buried in one of the St Isaac's crypts, but he was refused because of his non-Orthodoxy and his widow had to carry his coffin back to Paris.

IMPERIAL LYCÉE

On the outskirts of St Petersburg is Tsarskoe Selo, where the major tourist attraction is the Catherine Palace; few know that attached to the west wing is a gem of Classical stoicism, the Imperial Lycée. Opened at the end of the 18th century in the residence of Paul I's children, the Lycée offered the sons of the privileged a highly disciplined University-standard education in Greek, Latin, German, French, singing, fencing, drawing, physics, mathematics and politics. The 'Lycée-ists' then usually went on to serve in governmental or diplomatic posts.

Due to the later fame of one of its pupils, Alexander Pushkin, the Lycée has been preserved as a State Museum since 1949, and is therefore one of the few examples of a pre-Revolutionary school with classrooms. Pushkin, a student from 1811 to 1817, was renowned for being mischievous – just as he was in his adult life. His marks are on display in the museum, showing that he achieved bad grades in almost all subjects except French and Literature. Two of his classmates

were Pushchin and Küchelbecker, both of whom were later active in the Decembrist uprising, and caricatures of them drawn by Pushkin are also preserved.

Pushkin's parents were close friends with the inspired first Director, Vassily Malinovsky, whose political tract *Discourse on War and Peace* was one of the first publications to outline the principles of the United Nations. David de Boudry – brother of the revolutionary Jean-Paul Marat, but whose surname was changed by Catherine the Great – was French professor at the time and Alexander Kunitsyn, another author of 18th-century political works, taught moral sciences. Both professors were very much respected by the precocious Pushkin.

The Lycée had a maximum of 50 pupils from the families of the St Petersburg élite, and looking at the old registers one can recognize many names from Russian history. New candidates between the ages of 10 and 12 were accepted every three years, after four entrance exams. The boys wore uniforms and attended chapel services at the Catherine Palace with members of the

ABOVE: *Since this was a boarding school, each pupil had his own room – as well as his own valet. Pushkin's valet, Sazonov, was later found to have committed several murders and robberies during his period of service.*

LEFT: *The Hall: 'Between the columns in the Lycée Hall stood a table, always covered with a red cloth with gold trimmings. On this table always lay an Imperial Charter given to the Lycée.' Pushchin, 1812*

LEFT: *The gallery leading to the church in the Catherine Palace – the pupils were the only people outside the Imperial Court allowed to attend this church. The gallery walls are lined with bookshelves holding the works of great writers, philosophers and poets, including Homer, Virgil and Racine.*

BELOW: *The bedrooms lead off a regimented corridor.*

royal family and the Court. Most wealthy families had private tutors at home for their children, but the Lycée was an 'Internat' (boarding school). The discipline was strict but there was no corporal punishment, unlike most schools of that time, and each boy had his own valet. The Lycée became one of the most respected private education facilities of the 19th century and it soon outgrew this Classical building. In 1843 the school moved to larger premises in St Petersburg, where it remained until 1917.

During the Second World War the Nazis occupied the entire area of Tsarskoe Selo and they used the Lycée buildings as a hospital but, compared to the devastation they left elsewhere, there was very little damage to the interiors. The building later became a holiday home for Soviet writers, one of whom, Ansiferov, became the main researcher and advisor to the museum. On October 19 every year, there are now great festivities at the Lycée celebrating autumn and the beginning of the academic year. Famous guests visit and there are recitals and readings, ending in a firework display.

PUSHKIN'S APARTMENT

Alexander Sergeevich Pushkin is the literary idol of St Petersburg. The Soviet system accentuated the fact that he expressed the aspirations of a generation of revolutionary-minded nobility. Yes, he was a trouble-maker, continually playing pranks, constantly romancing other people's wives, and involved on the periphery of the Decembrist uprising. Later, he wrote verses that offended Tsar Nicholas I, who afterwards personally supervised his work. During Pushkin's short lifetime, he was exiled to the Caucasus, confined to his estate, harassed by the police and prevented from travelling abroad. Yet beyond all this he was a great romantic poet, with an insight on women that is rare in a man.

Pushkin's first success was *Ruslan and Ludmila*, an epic poem written when he was only twenty. Then came his great romantic novel in verse, *Eugene Onegin* (1823-31) – later adapted as an opera with music by Tchaikovsky – a historical tragedy, *Boris Godunov* (1825), also an opera, and *The Bronze Horseman* (1833), his much quoted tribute to St Petersburg. He also wrote prose such as *The Captain's Daughter* and *The Queen of Spades* and many short lyrical verses.

In the last year of his life, Pushkin was increasingly persecuted by the censors and his relations with Tsar Nicholas I and high society were strained. In November 1836, he received an anonymous letter hinting at an affair between his beautiful wife, Natalia, and the French roué, Georges d'Anthès. Despite being a philanderer himself, the hot-blooded Pushkin challenged the Baron to a duel. Early on January 27, 1837, he met his second, Danzas, in the Café of Wulf and Beranger and rode to the fatal spot on the Black River. He was mortally wounded, shot in the stomach and carried back to his rented apartment on the Moika in agony. For two days progress reports were hung from the window, as the great poet lay dying. At 2.45am on January 29 he died, and shortly afterwards Natalia left St Petersburg, never to return. Before the poet's possessions were removed from the 11-room apartment,

Zhukovsky, a contemporary of Pushkin's, drew a plan.

Since 1925, the apartment has been a memorial to Pushkin, restored with the help of Zhukovsky's drawing. Over the years, some of Pushkin's original possessions have been found: a walking stick with a button from Peter the Great's shirt inlaid in the handle, a bronze bell, an ivory knife, and a goose quill of the type Pushkin would have used. On the desk stands a New Year present given by his close friend, Nashchokin, who was famous for his eccentricity and wit: 'I am sending you your ancestor with an inkpot...' A bronze figurine of a black boy stands guarding the ink – Pushkin's great grandfather, Ibrahim Hannibal, was an Abyssinian brought to the Russian Court by Peter. To remind one that the poet died in this very room, his death mask, a locket with his hair and the waistcoat he wore on the day he was mortally wounded are also on display.

ABOVE: *Portrait of Alexander Puskin in 1827, by Orest Adamovich Kiprensky (1778-1836).*

OPPOSITE PAGE: *Pushkin's study, the room where he died on the divan from mortal wounds received in a duel. His library consisted of over 4,000 volumes in 14 languages. A contemporary described the study as 'spacious, light and clean, in the middle stood a large wooden desk, always covered with papers, letters and books, in the corner was a comfortable armchair in which the poet sat'.*

RIGHT: *The Literature Café, once known as the Café of Wulf and Beranger. It was here that Pushkin met his second, Danzas, before leaving to take part in the fatal duel.*

MADAME GOLOD'S APARTMENT

Hidden away behind a solid iron door, in a typical Petersburgian courtyard, there exists an exquisite example of Empire Classicism. It contains one of the finest collections of the century, but is not a museum – merely the moderate three-roomed apartment of Madame Golod. When invited for tea with the diminutive owner, I find her seated at the mahogany dining table clearing a game of patience, above her Grand Duchess Elena Pavlovna looks on serenely. I sit on a curved-back antique chair and begin to realize that every item in the room is a treasure. Small glass cabinets contain valuable ornaments, a French polished desk is covered in semi-precious stone boxes, a marble sculpture sits on a marble mantelpiece and there are two rows of miniatures on the wall. Madame Golod is obviously a woman of good taste.

Miniature painting is a specific form of art and portrait miniatures are a very special skill. These portraits were

widespread in Russia and Western European countries in the 18th and beginning of the 19th centuries. With so many arranged marriages, before photography the miniature was often the first view of a future spouse. A good artist could help hurry a union along! There were two forms of miniature: one enamelled and one the classical miniature, which used water-colour or gouache applied to ivory plates, parchment, or paper. This second form was easier and cheaper and therefore became more popular.

Miniatures were carefully framed for safe keeping, protecting the precious portrait – often the only memory of a husband at war, or a daughter who had married abroad. Now the significance of those pictured has passed, the rich frames have

ABOVE: *Every room of Madame Golod's modest 3-room flat is an exquisite example of Empire Classicism.*

LEFT: *Madame Golod made the bedhead herself, from an old mirror frame that had been broken in the war. It is strange to think of this frail, elderly woman living alone in such opulence, especially after she became a victim of the recent surge of crime, when a young, female robber made an attempt on her life. Fortunately the flat is well-protected and police rushed to the rescue.*

OPPOSITE PAGE: *In the Drawing Room, a collection of miniatures is displayed below a portrait of Grand Duchess Elena Pavlovna. The beaded cushions on the divan were sewn together from an old sweater. As one analyzes the length of Madame Golod's life, her ingenuity and great taste, it all seems less imposing and more just the home of a very cultured woman.*

added to their value. These intimate likenesses document historical changes in the style of hair, clothes and the faces themselves. Since the beginning of the 20th century, miniatures have been collected and exhibited, usually English, French and German. Less well known is the Russian school of painting. Madame Golod is known for her private collection, which includes several works by the outstanding artist Borovikovsky.

'I am not a collector,' she insists. Privileged visitors to her home must understand that she simply likes these things, and not ask questions as to how they have managed to remain intact throughout this eventful century. Madame Golod remembers

the Revolution, lived through the blockade of Leningrad and has recently suffered the effects of hyper inflation on her government pension, yet still she retains her precious possessions. Each has a story, a memory for their owner.

I realize that even after ten years of living in St Petersburg, there are still surprises for me. We have all become susceptible to the Soviet idea of 'Russia for the workers', and Western propaganda that has all Russians living in drab, shoebox-size apartments, with fitted plywood cupboards and flock wallpaper. Madame Golod is a reminder of St Petersburg's great past, which still exists for those with grace and style.

PHILHARMONIA

It is the music from St Petersburg, together with its literature and ballet, that first attracts many people to Russia. The beautiful Philharmonic Hall creates the perfect setting to listen to one of Tchaikovsky's symphonies or the dramatic Slavonic music of the Mighty Five (Borodin, Cui, Balakirev, Mussorgsky and Rimsky-Korsakov). Since 1974, the Philharmonia has been named after Dmitry Shostokovich, for it was in this hall that his heroic 7th Symphony (Leningrad) was performed in 1942 during the blockade of the city.

Until the 19th century, Russian music existed only as folk songs or religious choral music. From the 1730s, Italian chamber music was popular at court, until Catherine the Great encouraged a nationalistic movement from which Mikhail Glinka eventually emerged. He is considered the father of Russian music, but in Soviet times his opera *A Life for the Tsar* was regarded as an imperialist work and was renamed *Ivan Susanin*.

It is only since 1921 that this white Corinthian-columned hall, with its huge chandeliers, has been the home of the Philharmonic Orchestra. Before the Revolution, this was the Noble Assembly, described in a guide book to St Petersburg of 1887 as, 'the best club and the richest in the town'. This exclusive club was founded in 1835 by a Prince Dolgoruky, member of one of the oldest families in the Russian nobility, descendants of Rurik and founders of Moscow. Clearly, by its name, membership of the club was strictly limited to those with princely titles. This was a social place, for balls, parties and concerts. For the club, Paul Jacquot was commissioned to design 'a three tiered hall with excellent acoustics'; the façade was designed by Carlo Rossi, to blend with the Michael Palace ensemble on the opposite side of Arts Square.

The winter social season in St Petersburg began with a Christmas bazaar here, which lasted four days from 2pm until midnight with grand duchesses and princesses running stalls. The season would continue until Lent. Despite the cold weather, winter was when St Petersburg flourished, for in the summer months society left the city for the South of France, their summer palaces or to take the waters in Baden.

The smaller hall, known as the Mali, has existed since 1809. The premiere of Beethoven's *Missa Solemnis* was performed here in 1824, organized by Prince Nikolai Galitzine, one of the founders of the St Petersburg Philharmonic Society. The original score was presented to the Society and is kept in the library. Private concerts were often organized in the hall by the Imperial Russian Musical Society. This Society was set up in 1859 by Anton Rubinstein, then Principal of the Conservatory, under the patronage of Grand Duchess Elena Pavlovna, who was known as the muse Euterpe in musical circles. Adventurous programmes of contemporary Russian works were organized and Wagner, Liszt and Berlioz performed here. In 1893, nine days before his death, Tchaikovsky conducted his 6th Symphony, the *Pathétique*, for the first time. Modern historians note that it was met with a shocked silence, but in those days it would have been considered improper to applaud, as the quality of silence after a performance revealed the degree of its success. In fact members of the audience could be seen wiping away tears.

ABOVE: *The Director's Staircase, used by musicians, performers and special guests.*

RIGHT: *The private suite for the conductor, with balconies facing out over Ulitsa Mikhailovskaya. Here performers can receive guests after a concert.*

OPPOSITE PAGE: *The Shostokovich Hall provides a perfect setting for listening to great music. The resident orchestra is the St Petersburg Philharmonia under the brilliant conductor, Yuri Temirkanov.*

CENTRAL ARCHIVES

ABOVE: *Detail of a doorway in the Blue Hall, the work of Bosse in the 1840s, part of the main enfilade of rooms that face the Neva.*

LEFT: *The main staircase of the Laval House is enclosed under a circular rotunda, and the cupola is decorated with rosettes and stars.*

The grand arch that faces Decembrists' Square joins two buildings that once held the Senate, the Supreme Organ of the government of Russia, and the Holy Synod, the department of church affairs. The architect, Carlo Rossi, won a competition in 1829 to rebuild the old Senate building opposite the recently-finished Admiralty buildings by Zakharov. He was told to make his building reflect the large expanse of the square and the Senate and Synod were built in 1829-34 to his design.

Now these buildings – with the neighbouring Laval House bought by the Senate before the Revolution – house the Russian State Historical Archives. The Laval House first belonged to Menshikov, but after he had been exiled to Siberia in 1732 it became the residence of Vice Chancellor Ostermann. A decade later the Empress Elizabeth gave the house to General Saltykov and in 1790 the building was redesigned by Voronikhin for the Stroganovs. The interior seen today was designed by Thomas de Thomon for Countess Alexandra Laval in the early 19th century. At this time de Thomon was fashionable and expensive; the respectable French Count Laval had fallen on hard times, but the new Countess was from a wealthy family and so had full say in the style of the house. Her literary salons were filled with the big names of the day: Krylov, Zhukovsky, Griboedov, and Mickiewicz. Pushkin gave his first reading of *Boris Godunov* here, and Lermontov had a public quarrel with the Marquis de Barontes that led to a duel. The Laval's daughter, Ekaterina, married Prince Sergei Trubetskoy, the leader of the Decembrist group. Senate Square was renamed Decembrists' Square in 1925 in honour of the revolutionary gentry who rose up in arms against the Tsar for the first time in Russian history.

After the Senate and Synod were abolished in 1917, Lenin

decreed that archives should be collected in one place to protect Russian history. Now the Russian State Historical Archives in the former Senate, Synod and Laval buildings hold over 6,500,000 pre-Revolutionary documents, including Tsarist decrees on education, law and order, finance, trade and local administration. There are original scientific and architectural drawings, publications, letters, maps, engravings and much more. During my visit I saw the documents belonging to my great-grandfather detailing the sale of the Michael Palace, and the inventories and exhibition documents from the opening of the Imperial Russian Museum. There are also documents from the Heraldry Department of the Ruling Senate, and now a special office decides on membership of the nobility. Those making claims to noble birth can check here; one librarian told me how disappointed they are if told they have no claim. Files on Jewish affairs and the records reflecting the Tsarist government attitudes to Islam and Buddhism have only recently been made available to the general public. Still secret are old maps showing oil refineries, diamond and gold mines and some papers referring to citizenship. In the safes are metal engravings from Peter the Great's time and deeds important to Russian geographical history: details of the sale of Alaska and other proofs of boundaries. Access to these papers works under the old pass system and a document must be applied for, and fetched by a trained archivist. Only very recently have foreigners been allowed to apply for research passes.

ABOVE: *The Archives' Reading Room was once the ballroom, decorated in Pompeian style and with a balcony for musicians. It was designed by Charpentier, with polychrome ceiling paintings by Medici and Bezsonov. To enhance the feeling of space, mirrors under the arches reflect light from the windows opposite.*

LEFT: *The grand staircase of the Holy Synod. The patriarch ruled the Orthodox Church from within this building.*

OVERLEAF PAGE 82: *The building was bought by the Senate in 1912-14. After the Revolution, Lenin made a decree to collect all the archives as one, and the combination of the Senate and Synod buildings, including the Laval House, became the USSR Central State Historical Archives, home to over six million pre-Revolutionary documents. Those from 1917 onwards were taken to Moscow.*

THE ALCHEMY OF REFORM

IN THE MID-19TH CENTURY, against the backdrop of an expanding salon society in a city run by ineffectual government clerks as immortalized by Gogol, groups of conscious-stricken gentry began to criticize the State and the autocracy of the Tsar was questioned for the first time. Underground journals flourished and the first stirrings of socialist thought began. Since his reign had begun with the Decembrist uprising, a paranoid Nicholas I built a police state, creating a spy network and enforcing strict censorship that sowed the seeds of discontent amongst the emerging Russian intelligentsia. Another influence on society from the mid-1820s was the movement to assert a national identity – a revival of old Byzantine traditions in art and architecture. The new fashion in interior decor became known as 'La Style Russe' by the end of the century.

Toward the end of the 1850s, after a humiliating retreat in the Crimean War and the succession of Alexander II to the throne, Russia entered a period of change and uncertainty from which a path can be traced to the upheavals of 1917. An economy based on serfdom was hampering industrial change and a growing moral awareness among the noble classes eventually led to the emancipation of serfs in 1861, earning Alexander II the popular title 'The Tsar Liberator'. But the reforms did very little to satisfy the overall need for change which had been sparked by the intelligentsia; as a result revolutionary groups formed and, after seven attempts, the Tsar was assassinated by a terrorist wing of the populist party, The People's Will.

NEKRASOV'S APARTMENT

LEFT & ABOVE : *Nekrasov, one of the leading figures of the Realist School in Russian poetry, lived in this flat from the 1840s until his death in 1878. A painting by Ivan Kromskoy shows the venerable poet on his deathbed, and is displayed in a re-creation of the original room.*

Was Nikolai Nekrasov a great poet? This question was raised at his funeral, when Dostoevsky put him on a par with Pushkin and Lermontov. Some keen university student cried out, 'Higher!' and the debate has continued ever since. The first publication of Dostoevsky's *Poor Folk* in the review *St Petersburg Notes* was at the instigation of Nekrasov, and this may well have influenced the great author's praise. Everyone accepts that, during his lifetime, Nekrasov was a talented editor. After several years of writing reviews and cheap vaudeville ditties for the theatre, he acquired the journal *Sovremennik* (The Contemporary), begun by Pushkin in 1836. From 1846, Nekrasov and his co-editor, Panaev, received work from Turgenev, Tolstoy, Chernyshevsky, Saltykov-Shchedrin and other contemporary writers, and the journal became the foremost literary review of the time.

Nekrasov's spacious apartment on Liteiny Prospekt was laid out as both a home and an editorial office, and it became a nucleus for 19th-century progressive thinking. Ivan Panaev and his wife, Avdotya, lived in adjoining rooms to Nekrasov in a famous menâge à trois. Panaeva was an important Russian author in her own right; her work addressed radical issues such as the emancipation of women in Russia.

Sovremennik had a liberal outlook and looked at the leading political questions of the 1860s. After 20 years of Nekrasov's editorship, it was suspended by the authorities in 1866 after the first assassination attempt on Tsar Alexander II – who deemed its content too revolutionary. To save his career, Nekrasov wrote a poem in praise of Count Maravev, the most strict of government censors. Soon afterward, in 1868, Nekrasov became editor-in-chief of the other leading progressive journal, *Notes of the Fatherland*. Here was published his epic poem about the peasantry, *Who is Happy in Russia?*, in which seven peasants travel through the land in a fruitless search for a contented man.

He became more famous in Communist times after his death, due to Lenin's appreciation of his work. Lenin praised his exposé of the hardships of peasants under hypocritical and mean landlords. Nekrasov's poems concentrate on the mass of the Russian people and their sufferings – originally on the recommendation of the important critic Vissarion Belinsky, who was not impressed by Nekrasov's romantic works and advised him to choose his subject matter from contemporary Russia.

ABOVE LEFT: *The Nekrasov museum apartment was founded in 1946, 125 years after his birth. It contains many of the poet's personal belongings: a statuette of his favourite dog, his books, first editions, manuscripts, and several portraits of the time.*

LEFT & ABOVE RIGHT: *The son of a country squire, Nekrasov decorated his apartment to show his love of hunting. A stuffed bear, that once held a tray for visiting cards, stands at the entrance and there are other bears around as well as a large collection of stuffed wildfowl.*

Before the Emancipation of the Serfs:
To whom I like I mercy show,
And whom I like I kill;
My fist – my only constable,
My only law – my will.

After the Emancipation of the Serfs:
Oh true believing peasantry!
Russia's your mother small;
The Tsar's your little father,
And that for you is all.

NIKOLAI NEKRASOV

MARIINSKY PALACE

The Mariinsky Palace was built in 1839-44 by Andrei Stakenschneider for Tsar Nicholas I's favourite daughter, Maria, but in 1906-7 the interior was refurbished for the Offices of the State Council, the Duma. Facing St Isaac's Cathedral and bearing the medals won by the City in the Second World War, the building now accommodates the City Council. There are offices for the 50 deputies of the City Legislature, elected by direct vote; the deputies represent the various main parties, none of which has a majority, plus a few independents. The assembly is in session once or twice a week, to discuss the city budget and put controls on the spending of the City Governor's Office. At other times deputies meet voters or participate in the permanent commissions responsible for key issues of the city's life.

In Soviet times, city councils were created by the Communist Party to conceal the totalitarian regime. From the outside a normal democratic process seemed to exist, with election campaigns, votes and published results. In reality voters had no choice – there was only one candidate for every position. The results of Communist elections were impressive: usually 90% of registered voters turned out and 99.9% chose the Communist Party candidate! Councillors were chosen from trusted Party members, reliable workers, or Party activists; twice a year voting sessions were held, where the bills proposed by Party committees were automatically approved.

Shortly after I arrived in Leningrad in 1989, the first semi-democratic elections were held for a new Mayor. I remember remarking to my card-carrying landlady that it must be exciting for her to vote for the first time – she replied that in the USSR one had always voted! In fact the 1989 elections were the first to offer a choice of candidate since the 1920s, paving the way to democracy in Russia. I witnessed the demise of Communism and the dramatic coup of August 1991, when thousands gathered in St Isaac's and Palace Squares to protect the democratically elected City Council. My father came to Leningrad to witness the raising of the Tsarist flag over the Mariinsky Palace, something he never believed would happen

ABOVE: *The Gala Room overlooks St Isaac's Square and the rich dark red of the marble pilasters echoes the red granite colonnade of the cathedral opposite.*

OPPOSITE PAGE: *The Rotunda, a wonderfully light and delicate space rather like a Classical Greek temple.*

in his lifetime. Rostropovich, the exiled cellist, hired a plane to fly to Russia and give his support to the dramatic changes.

Democracy in Russia does not have an encouraging history; the first democratic institutions were only introduced at the very beginning of the 20th century and promptly removed a decade later. In following years the structure of the totalitarian state limited not only the opportunity for democracy itself, but information on the democratic process all over the world. Now Russia is in a learning stage, with new laws and codex appearing daily, while some antiquated Soviet laws still remain. A Russian citizen can now complain about the system without fear of arrest, although the feeble voice of under-funded pensioners still remains unheard.

CITY COURT

OPPOSITE PAGE TOP: *The wide white marble staircase, leading from the entrance to the apartments of the Chief of the Police on the first floor. A large mirror on the half-landing revealed who was arriving to those on the balcony above – this was a device used in the 19th century that has now been replaced by intercoms.*

LEFT: *The highly ornate Main Hall, with its massive chandelier shaped like a Tsar's crown, leads to a suite of apartments. This room is now used for lectures on law.*

T he City and Regional Court has been on the Fontanka since 1838, when it housed the dreaded IIIrd Department of His Majesty's Own Chancery – the political police that gained Nicholas I the reputation of being the gendarme of Europe. The Decembrist plot marking the start of his reign had made him wary of revolutionary tendencies, so the IIIrd Department was a secret police, a network of spies and informers compiling reports on political intrigues and strange goings-on, all of which Nicholas read. The reports were not just political; the extraordinary was also filed – a vision of the Holy Virgin in the village of Berezniki, a girl born to a simple family but given a boy's name by mistake, a dangerous dog in the neighbourhood. The IInd Department codified laws and its first chief, Mikhail

LEFT: *Detail of the ceiling of the Main Hall.*

Speransky, prepared the *Code of Laws of the Russian Empire* – a 15-volume work including all the laws and regulations in effect in Russia over the past 200 years.

The political police were dreaded as much as the Cheka and

KGB in Communist days. Both were unjust and cruel, both were created to defend a dictatorial system against all opposition. The chiefs could decide the fate of every Russian subject at will. People hated this building, which was referred to as the House by Chain Bridge. In the yard were 13 cells and Herzen, summoned there in 1840, wrote, 'Not everybody who had entered the gate of the house managed to get out, and those who did only went to Siberia or to the Alexeevsky Ravelin to find their deaths...' The police themselves had many ways of leaving the building, since it has several secret doors and staircases. Apparently there are five ways onto the street, and there is rumour of a tunnel leading to the Michael Fortress across the Fontanka, the entrance being through one of three doors now bricked up.

Held here were members of the nihilist group, 'The People's Will', immediately after they assassinated Tsar Alexander II by the Catherine Canal in 1881. Later the Church of the Resurrection of Christ, commonly known as the Church of Spilt Blood, was built where he fell. It was during Alexander's reign that the IIIrd Section was repressed and its name changed to the Okhrana. Judicial reform was introduced, creating magistrates' courts for each district and elective judges, but despite reforms and increased surveillance after many assassination attempts, the Tsar still died a violent death.

Alexander III continued to repress revolutionaries, and erected a complex for political prisoners, the Christy (Crosses), a large red-brick prison still used today for general criminals. By Nicholas II's time, the Okhrana dealt almost entirely with subversion and to travel abroad citizens had to apply here for foreign visas. Still revolutionaries flourished, and in 1917 the Okhrana chiefs were imprisoned in the Peter & Paul Fortress – and the days of the terrible Cheka began.

> *I saw a funny thing by Chain Bridge,*
> *The Devil laughing till his belly itched.*
> *Oh man! I can't believe it – Satan said –*
> *They study justice at the IIIrd Department*
> *Cheaters are teaching right from wrong, Oh My Lord!*
> *I think it is time I start teaching the Word...'*
>
> PETER SHUMAKHER

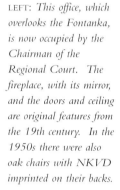

LEFT: *This office, which overlooks the Fontanka, is now occupied by the Chairman of the Regional Court. The fireplace, with its mirror, and the doors and ceiling are original features from the 19th century. In the 1950s there were also oak chairs with NKVD imprinted on their backs.*

OVERLEAF PAGES 90 TO 91: *In the Main Court Room, the cage is for criminals who may be a danger to society – this could mean numerous things in Soviet times. Recent famous trials include that of Yakubovsky, who stole rare manuscripts from the National Library.*

LEFT: *Fragment of a pre-Revolutionary wall fresco in the Court chapel. Many a prayer for redemption was no doubt offered in here.*

YUSUPOV PALACE ON LITEINY

The Yusupov family was one of the wealthiest in Russia, and they owned 43 of the grandest palaces across the country. In St Petersburg alone the family had seven palaces, all with the best addresses; the most well known is on the Moika, where Rasputin was murdered. The palace on Liteiny Prospekt was built in 1852 for the widowed Princess Zinaida Yusupova. Princess Zinaida, after a long affair with Tsar Nicholas I, left Russia and married a French Count, but the marriage contract stated that half her vast wealth must stay in Russia to be inherited by her son, Nicholas.

Prince Nicholas Yusupov had no sons, and his younger daughter, Tatyana, died at eighteen. The elder daughter, called Zinaida after her grandmother, became sole heiress to her father's fortune – and thus one of the richest prizes in the

ABOVE: *Malachite fireplace in the Director's office, formerly the boudoir of the Princess.*

LEFT: *The palace on Liteiny has a very feminine atmosphere. From the top of the stairs, visitors can be seen reflected in a mirror on the half-landing, which gave the hostess the opportunity to disappear if the guest was not welcome.*

marriage-market. Amongst her suitors were several Princes of reigning houses of Germany, but Princess Zinaida loved Russia too much to abandon it for a foreigner, even a Royal or a Serene Highness. She eventually married for love (which in these circles was rare at the time), her choice falling on an officer of the Chevalier Guards, Count Felix Sumarokov-Elston. When Prince Nicholas died the Yusupov title would have become extinct, but it was passed by Imperial permission to Zinaida's husband, who became Prince Yusupov, Count Sumarokov-Elston.

Their union was very happy and produced two sons, but the eldest, Nicholas, was killed in a duel by an officer of the Horse Guards. After his untimely death, Princess Zinaida led a retired life. All attention was focused on her wayward younger son, Felix - a handsome, daring man. After graduating from Oxford and tasting the high life in Paris, he married Irene, the niece of Tsar Nicholas II. On his marriage Felix received the right to the title of Prince Yusupov. It is Felix who is famous for his part in the murder of Rasputin in 1916.

During the First World War, the Princess made her palatial mansion into one of the best hospitals in Petrograd. The long hall on the ground floor was fitted up as a ward for soldiers with seventy beds. The operating room was equipped with all the newest surgical instruments and apparatus. Workshops were installed and instructors engaged to give invalid soldiers training in useful trades. Each patient received a complete outfit of clothes on leaving.

Princess Zinaida dealt personally with every detail of the hospital and spent a great deal of time there. She knew all the patients by name and she and her daughter-in-law, Princess Irene, lavished great care and attention on the wounded. Although the immense wealth of the hospital helped it become one of the most popular places to recover in, no amount of money could supply the atmosphere of love and kindness.

The present day curators are very proud of 'their' beautiful Zinaida and her golden heart. The house is currently used by the former Communist Party organisation Znaniye (Knowledge), which was set up to rehabilitate those who served in the Second World War. They now organize training programmes and cultural events.

LEFT: *Detail of plasterwork. The stuccoed walls had to be disinfected and painted white when the palace became a hospital - a small fortune was spent in adapting the apartments to make them appropriate for their new use. The ground floor was given up to soldiers, while officers occupied the first floor. Luxurious and cheerful sitting rooms were filled with hot-house plants and flowers; and there was a music room, reading room and grand dining room.*

LEFT: *The Rose Reception Room. The palace was built between 1852 and 1858 by Ludwig Bonstedt.*

FAR LEFT: *Detail of the ceiling of the Rose Reception Room.*

DOM ARCHITECTS

In Soviet Russia, the unions were allocated the palatial homes of the bourgeoisie as their headquarters. In 1934, the Architects' Union of Leningrad was given 52 Ulitsa Herzen, which they have restored over the years. Formerly the residence of the wealthy Polovtsov family, the building had been redesigned seven times as a private house before being adapted to the needs of the architects' club.

Before 1861, the house belonged to Prince Sergei Gagarin, Director of the Imperial Theatre. He had commissioned Alexander Pell, an assistant to Montferrand during the building of St Isaac's Cathedral, to rebuild an older house on the site. The exterior of the new house was in late Classical style, with an oriel window over the main entrance. In 1852 Prince Gagarin died, leaving unfinished refurbishment work. His son chose to live in No. 47 opposite, and No. 52 was bought in 1861 by the Court banker, Baron Alexander Stieglitz, as a wedding gift to his adopted daughter. Nadezhda Mikhailovna was her father's sole heir, and there is an apocryphal story that she was the illegitimate daughter of Grand Duke Michael Pavlovich and that the Tsar had personally asked Stieglitz to look after her. As a baby, she was left on the steps of Stone Island Palace with a note stating her name, patronymic and that she had been christened in June. She married Alexander Alexandrovich Polovtsov (1832-1909), an ambitious young clerk who rose to be Secretary of State in the Senate under Alexander III. Governor Polovtsov was also Chairman of the Russian Historical Society and meetings were held in the house in the beginning of the century.

Most of the interiors that remain today were commissioned by Polovtsov. He lived here whilst at the Senate, and through the young Gagarin opposite he met Maximilian Mesmakher, who was consequently appointed Director of his father-in-law's School for Technical Drawing. After the Baron's death, Polovtsov employed Mesmakher to build the Stieglitz Museum for his collection of Decorative Art and to redesign several rooms in his own home.

The building is filled with small touches of decorative

brilliance. The Dining Room, once the private dining hall of the Architects' Union but now a commercial restaurant, has walnut panels inlaid with Spanish Cordoba leather stamped with silver, dating from the time of the Inquisition. Rare

ABOVE: *The White Ballroom, by Bosse, is decorated in the style of Louis XV.*

BELOW: *Before bomb damage, the Oak Library designed by Bryullov was a third bigger and had two unique chandeliers – only one remains. The 16th-century Florentine mantelpiece was bought by Prince Gagarin for this room. The heavy oak doors are intricately decorated with carving, each square foot taking two masters six months. Each door weighs 300kgs, but can be opened and closed with the touch of a finger.*

LEFT: *The oriel window contained one of the most beautiful winter gardens in the city. The Polovtsovs filled it with rare orchids from the greenhouse at their dacha on Stone Island and people would stand on the street and stare up at the glorious plants.*

OVERLEAF PAGES 96 TO 97: *The Bronze Hall was originally a banqueting hall, with two manual lifts bringing hot food up from the kitchen. It was lit by natural daylight through a glass roof, or at night by gas lamps, which flickered dramatically on the different shades of bronze. The walls wee covered with valuable tapestries that had once hung in Napoleon's tent and were given by him to Alexander I. They are now in the Hermitage.*

BELOW: *The Bronze Hall is the best example of Mesmakher's Eclectic style. It utilizes almost every decorative technique, with tortoiseshell inlay, plaster mouldings, gold leaf, bronze railings, 32 types of wood, faux marble and mother of pearl. It was hit by a bomb during the Second World War and reconstructed as a lecture hall with cinema facilities.*

mosaics are hidden behind rich wall coverings in what was once a bathroom, and is now the Director's office.

In a report in 1943, Alexander Werth, the *Times* war correspondent, describes finding plans for the restoration of the city already laid out at the Union of Architects, although the war had not ended. I have found much of the material for this book in the library of the Architects' Union, as many an architect before me has found vital information when restoring an old palace. It is from their own archives that the architects of Leningrad have found the historical references to restore this building and, because it is their Union, such work was done with their heart and soul.

NEW MIKHAILOVSKY PALACE

On the Neva Embankment, with the most fabulous view of the Peter & Paul Fortress, is the huge palace of Grand Duke Mikhail Nikolaevich, fourth son of Nicholas I and youngest brother of Alexander II. During Alexander's reign, Grand Duke Mikhail was Viceroy to the Caucasus and, as well as this palace, he had a grand house in Tiflis and an estate, near Borjomi, roughly the size of Holland. The palace in the capital is big, but then so was his family – six sons and a daughter, who were brought up in strict military fashion. The Mikhailovich boys were known as 'the

ABOVE: *Much of the original decoration of the palace still survives – including the stamped leather wallcovering in this room that is decorated as a hunting lodge. It now serves as a lecture hall and the antiquated projector, which looks like something found on an archaeological dig, is still used regularly.*

LEFT: *The two great halls, one for dining, one for dancing, have 9m high ceilings, and the grand ballroom now houses over 30,000 books. The Neo-baroque Palace was taken over by institutions, and at present there are many establishments based in the premises: the Institute of the History of Material Culture (i.e. the Institute of Archaeology), the Institute of Eastern Studies, the Institute of Electronics Studies and a Japanese research firm involved in Buddhism.*

Caucasians' – used to growing up in the heat of the south they felt cold and uncomfortable on their visits to St Petersburg.

In March 1881, when the Tsar Liberator was assassinated on the banks of the Catherine Canal, it was Mikhail who saw to it that the dying Emperor was carried back to the Winter Palace. After his father's sudden death, Alexander III appointed Mikhail, his favourite uncle, President of the Council of State, bringing him back to live in the capital. The Grand Duke was very popular, for he was dignified and unpretentious. He lived through four reigns and remained influential, giving advice to

the last Tsar, Nicholas II. After his death in 1909 in Cannes, his body was brought back to Russia for a royal burial and laid to rest in the Peter & Paul Fortress. His son, Nikolai Mikhailovich, lived on in the empty palace, collecting butterflies and historical archives. His father had begun a collection of souvenirs from the Caucasus, and several halls on the ground floor, to the left of the main marble staircase, were open to the public.

Of the six sons, all Grand Dukes in their own right, three died at the hands of the Bolsheviks. Nikolai, a respected historian, and George, the Most August Manager (Chief Curator) of the Russian Museum of Emperor Alexander III, were arrested, imprisoned in the Peter & Paul Fortress and shot in January 1919. Grand Duke Sergei died in a mine shaft in Siberia in 1918. Alexander, married to Xenia, the Tsar's sister, escaped via the Caucasus. Alexei had died young and the remaining two children, Anastasia and Mikhail, were already married and living abroad – Mikhail in Kenwood House in London.

Now the huge palace houses many different organizations, and their workspaces and filing sit incongruously next to the elaborate original decor. Wandering around the vast expanse of the building, it seems inconceivable that just one family – even a family the size of Grand Duke Mikhail's – could ever have lived in such an enormous space.

RIGHT: *The former private chapel, with its unusual knotted columns, has been used since 1953 by the Chinese section of the Institute of Eastern Studies.*

FAR RIGHT: *The Grand Salon, in Neo-rococo style and overlooking the Neva, is now the reading room for the Library of Eastern Studies. Several of the sons had their own apartments and the distances in the building were so huge that Sergei, the Grand Duke's fourth son, would bicycle from one section to another. In one wing there was a swimming pool lined with artificial pink and green marble.*

RIGHT: *The New Mikhailovsky Palace was designed and built by Stakenschneider in 1863, and the unusual door handles are very typical examples of his detailing.*

MOORISH ROOMS

ince the split between the Orthodox Church and Constantinople, and because Russia's only Southern naval base is on the Black Sea, relations between Russia and Turkey were often poor. During the Russo-Turkish war of 1806-12 a Turk, Alexander Muruzi, spied on his country for Russia. As a reward he was given Russian citizenship by Tsar Alexander I in the 1880s, and after his death his family came to live in St Petersburg – bringing with them the exotic and colourful architecture of their former homeland. In 1874 they built an exquisite example of Moorish architecture on Liteiny Prospekt, which was designed by A.K. Serebryakov and began a craze for Moorish-style rooms throughout St Petersburg society. The brightly-patterned geometric tiles, gilding and elaborate carvings were also popular because they were reminiscent of the Alhambra Palace in Granada, and brought a welcome atmosphere of sunnier climes into the midst of the dark Russian winter.

Many palaces of this period have at least one Moorish room. The Moorish Boudoir in Grand Duke Vladimir's palace (now Dom Scientists) belonged to his wife, Grand Duchess Maria Pavlovna. It leads off Maria's study and, after the Classical French decor of her other rooms, its exuberant and colourful decoration comes as quite a surprise. The walls are of moulded stucco, in a design based on heavily stylized Islamic calligraphy with the lettering highlighted in gold, against a background of alternate red or blue. Inscriptions in both Arabic and Russian calligraphy run round the frieze. The room is furnished with low seating, which was originally covered in cashmere, and there are small tables of stained pear wood, painted in cinnabar and ultramarine, and little stools with tiny cushions. All the furniture was designed by Victor Shröeter, the talented assistant architect who worked on the main building.

Grand Duke Nicholas, son of Nicholas I, also had a Moorish Room in his palace. It was designed for his son, Peter, and formed part of his apartment in the southwest of the palace. The room is now unfurnished, and opens off the suite of offices of a trade union official – since 1917, the palace has

LEFT: *In Grand Duke Vladimir's Palace a gilded pine screen covers the window at one end of the room, which originally also had yellow satin hangings. The window looks out over the Neva river, towards the Peter & Paul Fortress.*

LEFT: *Detail of the alcove in the Moorish Boudoir of Malutka. The lower walls are covererd in a geometric mosaic made of small glazed tiles.*

OPPOSITE PAGE: *In Grand Duke Nicholas' Palace, the Moorish Room belonged to his son, Peter, and is a perfectly scaled down version of an Islamic prayer space. The domed ceiling has a bold raised pattern in blue edged with gold, against a red background. The ceiling design is based on typical Arabic geometric patterns.*

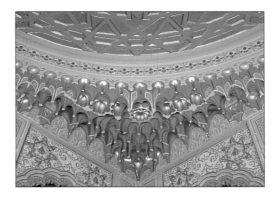

LEFT: *Corner of the ceiling of Grand Duke Peter's Moorish Room.*

been the headquarters of the trade union movement and was re-christened the Palace of Labour.

Possibly the most famous Moorish Room in St Petersburg is that in the Yusupov Palace on the Moika. The Yusupovs brought architects over from Spain to create it, and thus outdid all predecessors. It also ensured that the designs used were much more authentic – in many other cases Moorish, Persian, Islamic and Russian architectural elements were all combined together, just to give a rich and exotic effect.

ABOVE: *Detail of the ornate carving in the corner of the Moorish Room in the von Derwies house.*

RIGHT: *Arabic calligraphy was used entirely for decorative effect, with no thought as to its meaning. For example, in this room in the von Derwies house, words from the Qur'an were placed on the floor. This is offensive to Muslims, who will not step on the words of their Prophet.*

GRAND DUKE ALEXEI'S PALACE

Probably one of the most mysterious houses in St Petersburg is this sprawling residence on the Moika. Inside are empty walls, decaying interiors, no heating and no treasures – just ghosts from another age. Empty brass rings line the staircase, where in another life a plush carpet lay, guarding the white marble from the frequent tread of guests' feet. The doors are very large and firmly closed to visitors and it was only after two months of correct paperwork that we were eventually allowed in to photograph.

Grand Duke Alexei Alexandrovich was one of Tsar Nicholas II's influential uncles. When Alexander III died unexpectedly after a short reign, Nicholas was totally unprepared for the role of Emperor. He, therefore, turned frequently to his uncles, Vladimir, Alexei and Sergei, for advice. Paul, the youngest uncle, had been exiled to Paris for marrying a divorcée. Regardless of their knowledge or characters, the uncles were given positions of command in the Imperial Guard, the Navy and Moscow respectively.

Grand Duke Alexei was a sybarite, lounging around his suite of apartments in the Winter Palace and spending huge amounts of Treasury money travelling abroad in great luxury. When he became General Admiral of the Russian Navy, he felt it was time to get a place of his own. He bought several houses near the Anglisky Prospekt at the end of the Moika and

ABOVE: The Chinese Hall is decorated with ebony panelling in Chinoiserie geometric designs. The black ebony doors, with their engraved panels, must have been in sober contrast to the exotic Oriental pictures of dragons that the Grand Duke displayed to remind him of his Far Eastern travels.

RIGHT: Detail of the Grand Duke's monogram in one of the doors.

LEFT: The English Hall, with its complex plasterwork ceiling and oak doors, is in heavy Gothic style, which was very fashionable at the time. Soviet children once studied at a former institute in the palace, and one wonders what they made of their surroundings.

ABOVE: *The bathroom with bathing pool, the walls decorated with ceramic panels.*

ABOVE TOP: *The Grand Duke's Study has carved oak doors and a panelled ceiling. Under the gilt leather wall-covering the walls are lined with old newspaper covered in mildew and dated 1883 – the original date of the building.*

ABOVE: *The deserted library. All the rooms are empty, and they are all different sizes and styles.*

commissioned Mesmakher to convert, link and build anew, to create this amazing palace. Grand Duke Alexei loved fine food, good wines and attractive women, and he filled his new home with all three.

The building is extravagant in every sense of the word: two towers, a dining room and an ice room in the basement, a bathroom with a sunken bathing pool, semi-circular, square and oval windows, pilasters, decorative columns and carved banisters. The palace has no symmetry, it is a mélange of Roman, Gothic, Rococo, Baroque, Oriental and Classical styles, a typical example of the newly fashionable Eclectic wave. The main Dining Room has a stage with a dressing room and Alexei invited famous actors of the time to perform for his guests. He never allowed his house to be photographed, and the curator of the palace seems to be following this tradition; we were allowed to photograph only a few rooms and the others were kept locked in mystery.

Grand Duke Alexei never married, and when he died in 1909 the property was divided equally between two of his brothers and his nephew, Michael. None of them took much

interest in the palace, so Alexei was its first and last resident. Despite being used by Soviet institutions, his initials can still be found carved on wooden doors and in the wrought iron gates surrounding the park. It was said of the comfort-loving Duke that he was 'a man of infinite charm and enormous girth' and strangely, in the emptiness of the now deserted residence, something of his opulent spirit lives on.

POLOVTSOV DACHA

LEFT: *The marble staircase was made by Pavonazo. The painting on the half-landing shows Lenin talking to patients in the Winter Garden during his visit to the sanatorium with other elite Party members on July 19, 1920.*

OPPOSITE PAGE: *View from the main Vestibule, through the Central Hall and the White Column Hall, to the Winter Garden. The chandelier in the Central Hall was from the Michael Palace (now the Russian Museum), and the fireplace from the Michael Fortress.*

This most unlikely 'dacha' is on the far side of Stone Island. A grand Neo-classical mansion, it was built by architect Ivan Fomin in the shape of a Russian 'P' (π) for Alexander Alexandrovich Polovtsov. The final renovations, after seven years of building, were finished in 1916 – just in time for the Revolution. Hence this fabulously decorated and palatially furnished house became the first Workers' Sanatorium in Petrograd.

The land, with a wooden dacha, was a wedding gift from Baron Stieglitz to his beloved adopted daughter, Nadezhda and her husband, Governor Alexander Polovtsov. After his death in 1909, his son, also Alexander, decided to rebuild the old house. Neo-classicism was in vogue because of nationalistic hostility to the recent wave of European Art Nouveau and Austro-German Jugendstil, and the Polovtsov dacha was the grandest example of this hopeful revival of 19th-century Imperialism.

Following the angle of the original dacha, neither façade faces the Little Nevka river that runs nearby and separates the land from the Elagin Palace. The entrance has a portico with columns, flanked by symmetrical wings and the interior was opulently furnished; pieces from the original collection can now be found in the palaces of Gatchina and Elagin. Very valuable tapestries once hung in the Main Hall. They were

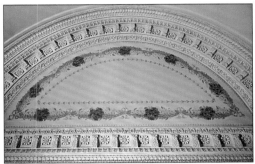

ABOVE TOP: *Detail of the polychrome paintings in the White Column Hall, which date back to the early 19th century.*

ABOVE: *The plafond in the bedroom was painted with beautiful poppies, representing sleep, by interior designer U.A. Bodaninsky. He also painted the friezes in the Tapestry Hall, and the large and small dining rooms.*

LEFT: *In the centre of the palace, the architect preserved some elements of the old dacha. The vaulted ceiling in the White Column Hall is made of oak beams from the former house. The Hall has Ionic columns and marble sculptures in niches, and leads into a romantic winter garden. Until the war, this garden was full of exotic plants, enveloping the Italian marble statues that stood among the palm trees.*

made in Belgium from paintings by Rubens, and somehow ended up in an auction in Stockholm in the 1930s. Interior designers were becoming fashionable, and Fomin's favourite was U.A. Bodaninsky, who painted many of the friezes.

Young Polovtsov saved no expense – his maternal grandfather had held the purse strings for the Tsar and Alexander Polovtsov Snr was once City Governor. With his first wife, he visited the dacha just for parties, holding great firework shows. In 1912, with the exterior complete, he spent the winter in the reconstructed house with close friends and his new wife, Sophie, a peasant girl to whom he played Pygmalion by

sending her to the Sorbonne and later marrying her. The interior took several more years to finish – with the outbreak of war and consequent scarcity of quality building supplies, the work was only finalised in 1916. Peter, Alexander's brother and Commandant for the Provisional Government of Petrograd in 1917, had his own suite of apartments. Sophie Polovtsova lived on Stone Island until 1918, when lack of fuel and heating supplies meant it became impossible to keep up. The couple escaped by foot across the border to Finland, and eventually reached Paris. Here Alexander Polovtsov, like many Russian émigrés including my own grandfather, opened an antique shop.

During the 1960s and 1970s, the mansion was a sanatorium for distressed women. Letters received from Paris in 1969, written by the ageing Sophie Polovtsova and describing the house in her day, were addressed to 'The Head Doctor of the Sanatorium Clinic on Stone Island that occupies the dacha that belonged to Polovtsov Junior'!

The house now stands empty and abandoned; few people know where to find it. In 1991, the mansion was rented out for 96 years to a young American businessman who hoped to create a business centre. But for the past five years, only the minimum wage has been paid to a skeleton staff and the contact number connects to 'Danny's Appliance Repairs Service' in New Jersey. Meanwhile the parquet made from nine different woods is buckling from damp, and the white interior has a grey, ruined look.

LEFT: *The painted ceiling in the Main Dining Room is very unusual, representing a stretched fabric ceiling with a lace overlay. A short corridor leads to a large kitchen, which was fully equipped for the 20th century and has never been modernized – despite having to cater for the residents of the sanatorium.*

RIGHT: *Even though the dacha has now been empty for many years, the Library still holds some books. This room was the location for the British Embassy in a US TV film on Catherine the Great. Double ebony doors given to Alexander Polovtsov Snr on completion of the Great Eastern Railroad, which his bank sponsored, are still standing.*

D.K. MAYAK

Dvoretz Kultura Mayak (Palace of Culture for Sailors) is in a most ornate house on Ulitsa Galernaya. Palaces of Culture are a product of the Soviet State, spacious buildings used by one particular group or profession. Unlike the House of Friendship, which encouraged meetings between foreigners and specially selected Soviet citizens, these 'community centres' were closely related to working life and aimed at people in their specific fields, encouraging them to work, rest and play together. In the large converted ballrooms of wealthy palaces lectures would be given, films shown and parties or celebrations held. The centres provided libraries and 'patriotic' recreation, such as folk dancing and amateur theatre groups. Due to the lack of space at home they became the centre of social life, and on Saturday nights sailors could bring their wives or girlfriends here for a night out.

Before the Revolution the house belonged to Sergei Pavlovich von Derwies, son of a rich railroad industrialist. Sergei loved the theatre and commissioned architect P. Shreiber to build an interior suitable for theatrical performances and musical receptions. At the end of the 1890s the White Hall was the venue for the Interlude fringe company, set up by the master-of-ceremonies, Boris Pronin (organizer of The Stray Dog Café), and Vsevolod Meyerhold — who worked under the pseudonym Doctor Dapertutto, a character in *Tales of Hoffman*. Meyerhold used this pseudonym for all his unofficial endeavours, as he was Stage Director of the Imperial Theatres. Interlude's repertoire included comedy, farce, pantomime, and vaudeville. Here Meyerhold made some of his first experiments with theatre, such as his macabre version of *Columbine's Scarf*, adapted from Schutzler's pantomime with actors approaching the stage from the audience and performances taking place simultaneously in various rooms. Stanislavsky, Chekhov and Vakhtangov were all known to have attended shows here. The White Hall was redecorated for a new owner, N. Shebeko, in 1909. He ran his own theatre, but in 1915 rented it out to a theatrical designer named Pollak.

Recently, on the same stage where Chaliapine sang and Isadora Duncan danced, transvestites performed daring drag shows on Friday nights. For Russia it is remarkable that such a club existed, as less than 10 years ago homosexuality was an offence, which could result in time spent in prison or a mental institution.

ABOVE: *Detail of the proscenium arch. The décor throughout the building is supremely frivolous, particularly in the theatre. Usually the buildings were redecorated with Communist symbols – Lenin's head, Marxist words of wisdom – but the theatre has retained its elaborate Rococo plasterwork from 1909, with caryatids and affectionate cherubs.*

LEFT: *The over-the-top decor lent itself to the camp performances of transvestites.*

OPPOSITE PAGE: *One of the few 'grotto' rooms left in St Petersburg, with moulded cement in stalactites around mirrors, and a mosaic floor. The doors once led to the winter garden, which no longer exists.*

MUKHINSKAYA ACADEMY OF ART

In Russia, 1879 was a time of great industrial change. To improve the aesthetics in industry and help Russia compete in the international market, Baron Alexander Ludwigovich Stieglitz commissioned Maximilian Mesmakher to create a technical drawing school, museum and library on the site of the all-Russian Industrial Exhibition of 1870. Baron Stieglitz was one of the richest men in Russia. He was so wealthy that he privately financed the Romanov family, and during the Russo-Turkish war he lent capital to foreign banks. He was also a great philanthropist, this school, museum and exhibition hall being the most permanent example of this.

The idea received the blessing of Tsar Alexander III, after he had viewed the museums complex in South Kensington, London. Mesmakher was a technical expert at building glass structures, hence the enormous roof over the exhibition space. He not only supervised the project, encouraging the use of Classical Palladian principles for the proportions, but was also the first Rector of the school.

The Museum of Decorative and Applied Arts was the first of its kind in Europe, and on opening it held 15,000 objects of interest – most drawn from the private collection of Stieglitz's son-in-law, Alexander Polovtsov. Exhibits covered a wide range of periods, displayed in rooms designed in a corresponding style. The central Exhibition Hall was the largest space in St Petersburg at the time and was used for special exhibitions. Tapestries and woven cloths were hung in the arches of the main floor and the gallery displayed Classical vases on each plinth. At the top of the stairs was a seated marble sculpture of the Baron by M. Antolkolsky, which was lost in Soviet times but recently discovered unharmed in Novgorod. Around the cornice below the gallery, medallions show great artists of the world.

In 1945 the building became the Mukhinskaya Institute of Art, named after Vera Mukhina, the socialist-realist sculptress famous for *Worker and Collective Farm Girl* in Moscow. The

ABOVE: *Detail of the painting on one of the pilasters in the Raphael Hall.*

LEFT: *The ceiling of the Raphael Hall is coffered and richly painted in Venetian Renaissance style, with designs by Saltikov and Bayinov inspired by St Mark's Library in Venice.*

LEFT: *The marble staircase leads from the upper to the lower galleries in the museum. The 'marble' walls are in fact scagliola. One wall is decorated with a quadratura wall painting of St Peter's in Rome by P.I. Dolgov.*

OVERLEAF PAGE 114: *The central Exhibition Hall is 34 x 17m and rises 22m into the enormous glass domed roof, a technical tour de force for the period designed by Maximilian Mesmakher. The plinths around the upper gallery once held Classical vases, while tropical plants and palms flourished on the lower level, protected by the glass from the harsh Russian winter.*

Institute mainly taught restoration and sculpture. Now it is the best known modern art school in Russia and has been renamed the Mukhinskaya Academy of Art. The massive Central Hall is still used for exhibitions and degree shows, while the museum has one of the largest collections of traditional Russian art. Restoration work on the various stylized halls throughout the building has been done by the students themselves.

INDUSTRIAL CHANGE

RUSSIA'S GREAT PERIOD OF INDUSTRIAL CHANGE began during the latter half of the 19th century. The majority of mansions in St Petersburg that stand today were built during this time, large family houses for the emerging middle classes and rich industrialists. The expansion of the railroads throughout Russia brought an awareness of other national cultures, especially from east of the Urals. This also led to wider trade and commerce and increased the wealth of the new bourgeoisie. The dominance of aristocratic Russia at last came to an end, suffocated by an upsurge of the merchant classes, financiers, industrialists and expanding commerce.

From the 1860s onwards, science attracted many young thinkers – men who were disinterested in politics yet keen to solve the problems of the world. They enabled Russia to make remarkable headway in the universal fields of scientific discovery. Alexander III encouraged a movement towards 'Russia for the Russians'. There was a new wave of interest in national culture, and a host of brilliant composers, musicians, painters, designers and writers from St Petersburg. The fashionable style was Russian Modern, based on the German Jugendstil. Although the rest of Russia remained unaffected by these influences, St Petersburg and Moscow were no longer culturally isolated from Europe.

INSTITUTE
OF ELECTRICITY

At the time of the Industrial Revolution, Russia was about ten years behind the rest of Europe – but made up for lost time with its brilliant scientists. Alexander Stepanovich Popov has five inventions to his name, including the radio and the lightning detector. In March 1896, Popov gave the first public demonstration of radio transmission and reception, several months before Marconi displayed his version to the world. The credit went to Marconi, as he thought to patent the idea whereas Popov went on to make other experiments. There is a saying in Russia today, that in science and industry the Russians invent a thing, the Americans market it and the Japanese sell it cheaper! The Popov radio is a classic example of the Russian attitude – proud of being the forerunner, but unconcerned about market value.

The pre-Revolutionary government, unlike the Soviet State, gave little funding to the sciences. Despite this, the Institute of Electricity was the first of its kind in the world, a purpose-built centre for the study and development of electricity. Built in 1900–3 by Alexander Vekshinsky, it is a red brick building in the Modern style. The Library has a large window almost covering an entire wall and surrounded by a mosaic frame on the exterior. The walls are lined with plaques honouring revolutionaries who studied at the Institute, supporting Lenin's theory that the Socialist Revolution would be successful only through the electrification of Russia.

The Institute is opposite Peter the Great's Botanical Gardens, quite far out from the city centre. This could explain why, at the end of the 19th century, the Archives of Interior Affairs were based here. Together with scientific secrets, state secrets were held in tight security. The original inventions of Popov and other leading Soviet scientists are kept in the decrepit storerooms of the Museum of Communication, opposite the Post Office, where the walls shift 5cm a year and the staff live in fear of the ceiling falling down again – as it did in 1974 on a group of visitors. After this catastrophe, the museum was closed for safety reasons and the valuable treasures it holds

LEFT: *Maquette of the 25m-high laboratory, built for conducting powerful electrical experiments – 1000 volts would sometimes be used, hence the need for such a height. In 1918, this was the most powerful generator in the world. The maquette is kept at the institute*

BELOW LEFT: *Due to lack of funding, even the Institute of Electricity cannot afford new light bulbs.*

BELOW: *Popov's radio, on display in the Museum of Communication.*

OPPOSITE PAGE LEFT: *Copies of the original inventions of Popov and other leading Soviet scientists on display in the small museum in the Institute of Electricity. The originals are in storage in the Museum of Communication.*

OPPOSITE PAGE RIGHT: *Popov's desk in the Institute of Electricity. His apartment is now a museum in a connecting building.*

were left to collect dust, occasionally being brought out for guests curious enough to ask. Such treasures of history, not just of Russia but of the world, may be lost forever when the roof caves in, unless the government manages to find the resources to invest in renovating the building. As some of the exhibits are now far too fragile or delicate to be moved to another location, their ultimate fate rests in the hands of the gods.

POST OFFICE

The Post Office is an entire region, with buildings on each side of Post Office Street connected by a famous covered gallery bearing the illuminated word 'POCHTAMT'. Various outbuildings housed the staff, the postmen and their transport – horses in stables or trucks in garages – and there were once hospitals, schools and a church. The area was known as the Post Office village. Peter the Great founded the Post Office in 1714, and in 1782 Catherine the Great moved it to New Isaac's Street, renaming it Post Office Street. From here, post coaches left for their long journeys across the Russian Empire, and milestones indicated their distance from this location. A letter sent from St Petersburg to the British envoy in Bukhara, Middle Asia, travelled non-stop all the way through each Russian province. At every post station, exhausted horses – or camels or reindeer, depending on the climate or region – would be exchanged.

The original building was a service centre; a courtyard with offices, stables and dormitories built by N.A. Lvov between 1782 and 1789. The ground floor had no windows, only niches for sculptures that were never installed, but when architect Y.T. Sokolov refurbished the building in 1801-3, windows were added. In 1829, the Post Office bought the Bezborodko mansion diagonally opposite. Bezborodko was Catherine the Great's brilliant clerk, found in the Ukraine by Potemkin and brought to St Petersburg because of his fantastic memory. Here he lived a debauched and disreputable life, but despite excessive drinking managed to keep his memory skills. In his mansion, an oval room with a false ceiling hides an upper level decorated with butterflies. Rumour has it that this was a Masonic Lodge, and the coffin used in one of the ceremonies would be lowered through the access hole. This, and the neighbouring building, were refashioned by Giacomo Quarenghi to provide a church and extended quarters for Post Office workers. This building is now the Museum of Communication. The famous closed gallery across Post Office Street was built in 1859, to connect yet another building. The architect, Albert Kavos, was a student of Carlo Rossi and also built post offices in Peterhof and Moscow.

The post office system in Russia is responsible for communications, including mail, telegrams, and subscriptions for newspapers and magazines. In Soviet times, it also covered intercity telephone calls, thus having complete control over any exchange of information. Special readers were employed for letters in foreign languages; their offices on the second floor were once the 'Black Offices' of the Tsarist censors working for the Okhrana. With only ten employees, not every letter could be read and the vast majority ended up in the bin – perhaps one of the main reasons for Russia's renowned inefficient postal service. People, out of habit, still prefer to have foreign letters hand-delivered.

In 1857 the first stamp was produced; later each region (Zemstvo) provided its own postal service and these stamps became a specialist field for collectors. The Museum of Communication was recently presented with leather-bound volumes holding Tsar Nicholas II's personal stamp collection from 1913, including stamps celebrating the 300-year centenary of the Romanov dynasty, which are renowned for their intricate engraving. He supposedly took these albums to Ekaterinburg in 1918, from where they disappeared after his murder. Soviet stamps have always been very elaborate, with several new pictorial series each month, making them charming to collect but not necessarily serving their purpose of getting letters to their destination.

ABOVE: *The covered gallery over Post Office Street.*

OPPOSITE PAGE: *This massive glass hall is only part of the extensive Central Post Office complex. You can not only buy stamps here, but also send items by Federal Express and Russian Federation registered post, and there is a counter for philatelists and for professional parcel packing.*

TELEPHONE EXCHANGE

The first telephone in St Petersburg was installed in 1882, and by July of that year 126 numbers were connected in central locations around the city – mainly in the Ministry of the Interior and other military organizations. Of these original lines, only 50 could be used simultaneously. After the live transmission of an opera, via a telephone at the Electric Technical Exhibition, the demand for telephones grew rapidly. Banks, the Stock Exchange, railroad stations and factories realized the importance of such direct communication, and by October 1882 the number of lines had doubled. By 1888, there was already a telephone directory with street maps, listing organizations and private houses with telephones. These directories can sometimes still be found in antique book shops; on looking up my grandmother's address I found they had telephone number 18 – one of the first private numbers! Telephones were a status symbol, and designed to blend in with interiors.

The telephone exchange employed young girls; they had to be under the age of 30, single, of a certain height, and with long arms. This was so that their heads were not full of domestic problems and they could reach the full length of the wooden exchange. Some of these original wooden boards can be seen in the Museum of Communication. The girls wore

LEFT: *Art Nouveau, as opposed to the more common Russian Modern, is rarely found in Russia in such perfect condition.*

OPPOSITE PAGE: *The telephone exchange is in the fine interior of the Azovsko-Donskoy Bank, which was designed by Lidval. Once it was filled with people waiting to make international calls, but these days it is easier to telephone from home.*

BELOW: *In the entrance stands a marble statue of Venus, and the custom was to rub her foot on leaving and make a wish. For many, the wishes made on Venus' foot have come true.*

uniforms of black skirt and white shirt.

Since 1935-7, the international telephone and telegraph exchange of Leningrad has been located in a building on Bolshaya Morskaya, not far from the General Staff Arch that faces Palace Square. The building was designed in 1908 by Feodor Lidval (architect of the Grand Hotel Europe and the Astoria) and was originally the Azovsko-Donskoy Bank. This was one of the new affluent banks that had sprung up after the expansion of the railroads and the development of world interest in Russian natural resources. The Director of the Bank in 1914, Count Ambrose Saramanger, lived in great style on the Fontanka and, no doubt, was the pre-Revolutionary equivalent of the wealthy 'New Russians' of today.

In the Cold War years, this exchange offered the only means of telephoning another country, although the place was under constant observation and calls were screened. To make a call abroad one would set the whole day aside, placing an order for a connection in advance and being prepared to wait several hours. Now such calls can be made from home so the place is somewhat empty, but in those days it was always crowded and often a good meeting point for those with cosmopolitan ideas.

The city now has many competitors vying for custom and the St Petersburg Telephone Exchange offers fax and internet services, as well as intercity and international connections. The main hall is full of memories, and the grand interior is all that remains to remind users of more difficult times.

GRAND HOTEL EUROPE

From the time of Peter the Great, the city has needed hotels. The first, the Austeria, was a hostelry for Peter's guests near his domik on Petrogradsky Island. Later, inns and taverns opened for traders and visitors to the city. Ulitsa Mikhailovskaya, where the Grand Hotel Europe now stands, was initially a marshy river into which merchants from Gostiny Dvor bazaar threw their debris. Eventually it was filled in and the area was developed by architect Mikhail Zemtsov, but it was not until Carlo Rossi built the Michael Palace (now the Russian Museum) in 1819-25 that this part of the city became an architectural ensemble. In 1834, Nicholas I – who had to approve every building plan – agreed to a unified façade for the street.

There was already a noteworthy tavern on Ulitsa Mikhailovskaya run by a degenerate French innkeeper, Monsieur Coulon. The Marquis de Custine describes it as 'filled with bugs and stifling hot and unwelcoming, but full due to the marriage of the Grand Duchess Maria Nikolaevna'. Mr Klee, a German, joined Coulon, and the hotel became known as Coulon and Klee's, or simply Hotel de l'Europe. The hotel restaurant was a meeting place for writers and artists; Dostoevsky dined with Turgenev when the latter was a guest, and Taras Shevchenko attended Bryullov's wedding reception dinner here.

In 1875, Gorky notes the opening of a new hotel on the corner of Nevsky Prospekt and Ulitsa Mikhailovskaya in one of his short stories. By 1873, a company of wealthy businessmen had bought up one side of Ulitsa Mikhailovskaya and hired architect L.F. Fontana to create a large hotel. It had electric light, lifts, a wine cellar, 14 carriages and 260 rooms, each fitted with airbells to call the staff. The kitchen and laundry were on the top floors, so that no unpleasant smells filtered through the building. The doormen wore Cossack uniform, and the restaurant staff were Tartars – men noted for their cleanliness, honesty and sobriety.

During the First World War, the hotel gave its rooms to foreign aid services. After the Revolution, it became the

LEFT: *When the hotel was refurbished, research was done into original furnishings and fittings so they could be recreated. The art nouveau bar was originally designed by Feodor Lidval in 1907-14. He was also the designer of the Hotel Astoria, opened as a rival to the Europe in 1912.*

LEFT: *Dostoevsky described the décor as representing a new trend in Russian society, showing the influence of America and the businessmen's credo.*

House of Soviet Clerks, an orphanage for victims of the Revolution and temporary housing for those waiting for new apartments. Families were crammed with all their possessions in rooms that now cost over $300 a night. Later, the Intourist Hotel Europe, with its dark corners, was the perfect place for surreptitious meetings and illicit money-changing deals – and was watched by the NKVD. The restaurant was limited to eleven Soviet hotel prostitutes, who were chosen for their command of languages. They earned 1,000 roubles a month – 50 times more than a factory worker.

In 1989, the hotel was closed for complete refurbishment and when the Grand Hotel Europe re-opened in a new Russia, it received 5 stars. Film stars and supermodels have stayed there – as well as HRH Charles, Prince of Wales,

who commandeered a whole floor. In 1995, it became the first Russian hotel to be included in Leading Hotels in the World and the following year made the list of Most Famous Hotels in the World. For everyone in the city, it is a civilized sanctuary from the pressure of Nevsky Prospekt.

ABOVE: *The Europe restaurant has recently been restored to the 1905 design of K. McKenzie. Electric light bulbs were such a novelty and a luxury at this time, that they were used as a decorative feature rather than being hidden away. The original stained glass panel, Apollo in a Chariot, was designed by McKenzie and made by M. Franck & Company.*

VITEBSKY STATION

The first experimental railway track in Russia – 22km between St Petersburg and Pavlovsk – was laid by the Viennese engineer F.A. von Gerstner, and the first train journey was on October 30, 1837. One of the passengers on the steam train wrote of his impressions in a St Petersburg newspaper, saying that on the return run the train made 'almost a verst (1.06km) a minute ... 60 versts per hour: horrible thought! Meanwhile, you sit calmly, you do not notice this speed that terrifies the imagination, only the wind whistles, only the "steed" breathes fiery foam, leaving a white cloud of steam in its wake.'

To encourage people to visit Pavlovsk by train, a concert hall was built next door to the terminus there. It was named after the Vauxhall Pleasure Gardens in London, and became famous for its popular evening concerts in the summer. People would say to one another, 'I am going to the Vauxhall!' and soon the word became synonymous with a railway station and earned its place in the Russian language. The hall became Petersburg's musical oasis, and home of the first Russian Philharmonic Society. The Pavlovsk Vauxhall was destroyed during the Second World War, and because none of the original designs could be found it was impossible to restore.

Vitebsky Station is built on the site of the first wooden station, the St Petersburg terminus for the railway to Tsarskoe Selo. The initial railway tickets were punch-stamped brass plates and, during the first months, the steam-powered trains ran only on Sundays and holidays – on weekdays, the locomotives rested and the carriages were pulled by teams of horses. By the summer of 1838, steam engines served as motors in factories, as well as on the railroads, and in 1851 the Nicholas Railway, between St Petersburg and Moscow, was built. The Crimean War showed the strategic importance of a railway network in coping with enormous distances, and by the late 1880s 21,000 versts of railroad crossed the vast expanses of Russia.

Alexander III bought his imperial train with luxury carriages from Napoleon III, although it had to be greatly enlarged to fit the Russian gauge, which was 5'6" wide compared to the standard European gauge of 4'8½". The imperial train used by Nicholas II was described in the memoirs of General Count Alexander Grabbe: 'Curiously enough the train had a duplicate, which outwardly was identical. As a precaution one travelled ahead of the other, and no one was told, not even the railroad administration, which one came first. The imperial train was a glistening deep blue, and had a small gold monogram – NII – on its doors. The Tsar used the train for various trips to the front. Before the war, it had been mainly used for the long journey to the Crimea.' It was while Nicholas was travelling in this train, to inspect troops in Mogilev, that he was forced to abdicate in Dno in March 1917. That April Lenin arrived in Petrograd from Zurich, sponsored by the Germans in the hope that his presence would further destabilize Russia. Since he was a Russian citizen and could not officially cross German borders in wartime, he travelled in a sealed railway coach. Lenin's carriage is displayed in a glass case in Finland Station. Similarly one of the first steam trains is on show at Vitebsky Station.

OPPOSITE PAGE: *Built in 1902-4, the Tsarskoe Selo railway terminal – now known as Vitebsky Station – was one of the most significant new constructions of the expanding railway system. More recently, a Hollywood production of* Anna Karenina *used this station inappropriately as the fateful place of Anna's suicide.*

ABOVE: *The architects, S. Brzozowski and S. Minash, built an Eclectic exterior, which conceals grand halls and staircases decorated with Art Nouveau and Jugendstil motifs in the finest marble and bronze.*

OVERLEAF PAGES 126 TO 127: *This exuberant Art Nouveau panel divides the waiting room from the adjacent restaurant, which has recently been restored to its luxurious pre-Revolutionary style.*

BELOW: *One of the large Art Nouveau waiting rooms, with paintings of Tsarskoe Selo and Vitebsk – the town from which this station takes its name.*

ELISEEV SHOP, GASTRONOM No.1

A huge granite building dominates the corner of Nevsky Prospekt and Malaya Sadovaya. This was the Eliseev Brothers Trading House Company, designed by architect Gabriel Baranovsky in 1902-3 and one of the first in a wave of modernist buildings that changed the face of St Petersburg. The building had several functions – the ground floor was a food hall, above it was a theatre and on the top floor there was a restaurant. All were decorated in the eclectic Modern style, the solid dark granite contrasting with delicate lacy metalwork and brightly coloured flowers in stained glass. On the exterior, dark bronze allegorical figures loom at each corner representing Industry, Trade, Art and the Sciences – the four elements contained within this extravagant complex.

The Eliseev family began building their fortune by selling pies on Nevsky Prospekt. Later their descendants became the richest merchants in Russia, second only to the Apraksin family, and well-known around the world through their trade links with countries such as France, England, Germany, Italy, and Spain. When their shop opened, St Petersburg was the richest capital in Europe and the food hall sold luxury foods and wines to the aristocracy, its elaborate décor accentuating

the opulence of its products. Whole harvests of French wine were bought up by the company and put into stock. Ice from the Neva in winter was used to preserve the freshness of goods brought in from all over the world. The basement storage space stretched beyond the building and under the courtyard outside, housing its own bakery and laundry to service the building.

In the dreadful Siege of Leningrad in 1941-4 this basement store helped to feed many citizens. Eliseev's – as it was still known although it had been officially renamed Gastronom No. 1 by the Soviets - became once again an élite foodstore – but this time feeding the artists, actors and journalists responsible for saving Russian culture. They were issued with special coupons and prices were cheaper for them.

After the war the cash tills were placed in the centre, very high up and lit by candelabra, giving the effect of a central beacon. The main vitrine and stained glass windows had been badly damaged and were carefully rebuilt. In the last five years the shop has been completely restored: the central tills were removed, and the food hall has been returned almost to its original splendour. The gold decoration is 24-carat gold leaf, applied using traditional techniques – although at floor level where there was once a real bronze wainscot, there is now a metal copy because of the cost. The lights are bright, the mirror shines, foreign food products are back on the shelves, and Eliseev's is once again a commercial trading house with a chain of stores – in which you can also buy shares in the St Petersburg Stock Exchange.

ABOVE: *Detail of the stained glass windows, which were destroyed during the Siege of Leningrad and were carefully restored by skilled craftsmen after the war.*

LEFT: *The original art nouveau lily lamps, destroyed during the war, were designed by Gabriel Baranovsky. They have been copied from old photographs and painstakingly rebuilt by one craftswoman, Vera Mikheikina.*

OPPOSITE PAGE: *At the rear of the shop is a massive mirror in the Modern style, with a delicate metalwork balcony above. All the gold decoration is in 24-carat gold leaf.*

LEFT: *View of the food hall looking towards Nevsky Prospekt, showing the elaborate stained glass windows.*

PHARMACY

The first pharmacy in St Petersburg, built by Trezzini, was on Aptekarsky Pereulok (Apteka means chemist). From here, herbal cures grown in the Apothecary Gardens were distributed. Peter the Great picked up training in medicine and surgery abroad, often practising what he learnt on his subjects, and opened the first hospital in 1706. Catherine the Great employed a personal English doctor, Dr Dimsdale, and was the first in Russia to be inoculated against smallpox. During her reign, she opened hospitals and encouraged Russians to learn medicine.

The nobility had their own apothecaries and doctors – usually foreign – and quacks were continually appearing in St Petersburg society. Before Grigory Rasputin, Empress Alexandra placed her faith in Philippe of Lyons to select the sex of her next child through psychic fluids; unfortunately he was wrong twice and was dismissed. Nicholas consulted Dr Badmaev, who prescribed hashish and henbane tea as an old Mongolian remedy; Felix Yusupov believed it was making the Tsar into a complete cretin. Ordinary people made do with folk medicine and herbs – Siberian herbal cures are as diverse as those in Chinese medicine.

In Soviet times the best hospitals served the military, but Russian health care is now opening up to the private market. Highly qualified surgeons and doctors are offered posts in Western-style clinics and no longer have to go abroad for better

ABOVE TOP: *A cash-till from another epoch. According to a guide book dated 1887 a consultation at this pharmacy cost 30 kopecks, but was free for the poor. In the 1930s, an intellectual would have to wait until all the workers had been treated.*

ABOVE: *The composer Borodin was a chemist and Stravinsky a hypochondriac. One wrote music between taking pills, the other took pills between writing music. No one can explain the tradition in Russia of having an alligator hanging in the pharmacy*

OPPPOSITE PAGE: *The interior of the pharmacy that served the Romanov Court, A. Poehl and Sons. Doctor Poehl was a pharmacist, chemist and graduate of philosophy, and he invented a number of organic treatments still used today. A century ago medicines were made up in a laboratory on the premises, making it one of the first homoeopathic dispensaries in Russia, and the equipment used is displayed on the shelves. The shop still operates as a chemist, but is also a museum — if requested the head pharmacist will recount the history of pharmacology in Russia.*

All East European Socialist countries were members of the Sovet Ekonomicheskoj Vzaimopomoschi (Council for Economic Collaboration) or SEV, the Communist equivalent to the EEC. Based in Moscow, SEV planned the economic development of member countries. The policy was to keep the key industries inside the Soviet Union, giving the East European countries only light industries to develop so they were dependant on Soviet supplies. Thus the pharmaceutical industry was based in Hungary, Czechoslovakia and Bulgaria and almost all its output was exported to the Soviet Union. After the collapse of Communism, a market economy developed and the East European countries lost their lead position in the market as more affordable — but often inferior — medicines made in India and Turkey became available. As time passed, reasonable concerns were raised about their quality. All major pharmaceutical manufacturers now target Russia, conducting massive advertising campaigns and introducing new medicines. Russians have grown up knowing East European drugs, however, so there is good reason for these countries, unable to compete in the European market, to come back to Russia with their medicines.

jobs. Some of the world's top surgeons are from the former Soviet Union — Feodorov the eye surgeon, for example, tours the world performing laser surgery. Only a small percentage of the Russian population can afford to pay for healthcare, however, and ordinary people often have to provide their own medicines (including syringes) before going into hospital.

Drug companies are offloading older products onto the Russian market, so suddenly pharmacies are flooded with Western packaging. This confuses the babushkas, who do not speak English and rely on familiar Czech cures. Chemists are very hit or miss — they seem to display an enormous range of drugs, but never have the one you need. The pharmacist is always very helpful on where else a product might be found, but this is no guarantee of success.

'Holy Russia' as a whole was untouched by scientific life and possessed knowledge that is not to be found through the laboratory. The best Russian remedy I ever tried was for migraine: I was advised to place the broken leaves of a cold cabbage on my head, put on wet cotton socks covered by thick dry woollen ones, take 2 teaspoons of honey and go to bed. And it worked!

ETHNOGRAPHIC MUSEUM

In 1895, Nicholas II issued a decree to found a Russian Museum in memory of his father, Alexander III. There were three main departments: Russian fine arts, applied arts and crafts and ethnography. The building chosen for the new museum was the Michael Palace, built by Carlo Rossi in 1819-25 for the youngest son of Paul I, Grand Duke Michael Pavlovich. His grandson was my great-grandfather, Duke George Mecklenburg-Strelitz, who in 1895 was ordered to sell the family home for five million gold roubles – a vast sum. The interiors were refitted to house the museum's collection by architect Vassily Svinin.

Alexander III had intended to create a centre for Russian culture; his motto was 'Russia for the Russians' and during his reign there was a marked tendency towards Russification – St Petersburg had become too Europeanized, like an island disconnected from the rest of Russia. He encouraged the speaking of Russian at Court, rather than French, changed army uniforms to the old caftan style and wore a beard – the first Tsar to do so, since Peter the Great went round chopping off facial hair.

Tsar Nicholas II donated exhibits from Gatchina and Tsarskoe Selo, gifts presented to the Imperial family from all

LEFT: *Svinin followed the Greco-Roman traditions of a peristyle for the pink Marble Hall, originally built as a Memorial Hall for Alexander III. Made from pink Karelian marble, the columns were produced at a processing plant built in the city, the first of its kind in Russia. A bronze tracery pattern runs around the perimeter of the ceiling and the plafond of crystal slabs is etched with double-headed eagles and oak leaves. The Marble Hall covers 935sqm, and it was badly damaged in the Second World War. The glass ceiling was replaced in parts, but the new glass is not nearly as elaborate as Svinin's original panes – some of which can still be seen, looking darker than the new glass.*

over the Russian Empire; he also bought collections of Russian antiques to donate to the museum. In 1903, to increase 'Society's' interest in their national heritage, he hosted a masquerade ball at the Winter Palace, the theme of which was late 17th-century Russian dress. Other collections were donated by Grand Duke Nicholas Nikolaevich Jnr, who had a fine collection from the East and the Balkans, and his uncle, Grand Duke Mikhail Nikolaevich, who was Governor-General to the Caucasus between 1862 and 1865. The latter's third son, George Mikhailovich, was first Most August Manager of the Museum until he was arrested in 1917. He donated his collection of coins and rare books, as well as cataloguing the collection. After the Revolution many new exhibits appeared, appropriated by the State.

The Ethnographic Museum is situated in a separate wing, which was added by Svinin in 1913 on the site of the old stables and laundry. This wing was originally supposed to house a Memorial Department, which was to be devoted to the memory of Alexander III. This department was never opened due to political events, but after the Revolution, in 1923, it was here that the first ethnographic exhibition was held to coincide with the creation of the Union of Soviet Socialist Republics.

Svinin tried to create an alliance between the Classicism of the Rossi palace and the new purpose-built museum. The Memorial Hall was intended to house a monument to Alexander III, with galleries behind the colonnade. Before his death, this very Russian Tsar had approved the original project, with a proviso that only Russian materials and labour could be used in the building. To create the Bohemian glass roof, Russian workers loaded with Russian sand were sent to Bohemia to learn their methods, thus not breaking the Tsar's command.

RIGHT: *The Grand Entrance, built to blend with the Classical Rossi palace next door. The museum encourages Russians to understand the wealth of different cultures in their country. It contains costumes, utensils and the recreated homes of each national type of the former Russian Empire/Soviet Union.*

OVERLEAF PAGES 134 TO 135: *A high relief, sculpted by M. Kharmalov and V. Bogatyrov, lines three of the walls of the Marble Hall. It depicts the Russian people and scenes from their everyday lives, but was never cast in bronze and so remains in plaster, coloured to look like metal.*

BUDDHIST TEMPLE

The history of Buddhism in Russia dates back to the late 17th century, when Buddhist teachers came from Tibet and Mongolia to the lands beyond Lake Baikal – Tuva, Buryat and Kalmiky. As the faith of Buddhism spread and new monasteries were founded, the Russian government legally acknowledged the religion in these areas. By 1741

ABOVE & LEFT:
The original symbols and elements were created in Eastern Tibet and given to the temple in 1915, to celebrate its consecration, but in 1919 the temple was ransacked by 'barbarians' and much was lost forever. The temple is being restored with the help of donations from Buddhist monasteries around the world.

there was an officially recognized Buryat Lama.

The temple in St Petersburg was the first in Europe, built to provide a base for the Dalai Lama in Russia. Most of the Buddhist architecture beyond Lake Baikal took its influence from Mongolian and Chinese style, but the temple in St Petersburg is a mix of authentic Tibetan architecture and the elegant Russian Modern style, built in granite with glazed brick and golden decorative details. Designed by Gabriel V. Baranovsky, the building was commissioned with the agreement of Tsar Nicholas II in 1909, after the Russo-Japanese war (1904-5) and the British invasion of Lhasa (the forbidden city of Tibet) in 1904. The project was supervised by Agvan Lobsan Derzhiev, the highly respected Buryat Lama. He had received his religious training in the Drepung monastery (one of the largest in the world) and was an instructor to the Dalai Lama XIII. The committee for the building project included many famous people of the time with an interest in Eastern culture, including Grand Duke Konstantine, Dr Badmaev (Tsar Nicholas II's advisor), Prince Ukhtomsky, and artists Roerich and Schneider. Present at the opening in 1915 were the Dalai Lama XIII, King Rama IV of Siam (of *King and I* fame) and representatives from the Russian government.

In 1919, the first Buddhist exhibition was held and that same year the temple was ransacked by 'barbarians'. Agvan Derzhiev tried to restore what he could, even in the difficult post-Revolution economic period, but most was lost forever. With the onset of anti-religious laws, by 1929 most of the Buddhist monasteries had collapsed. Like the followers of every other religion, Buddhists suffered under repression and by 1937, because of so many arrests and murders of the congregation, the temple had ceased to function. That November, the eighty-year-old Agvan Derzhiev was arrested in Buryat for his beliefs and died shortly afterwards in a prison hospital in Ulan-Ude.

During the Siege of Leningrad, in the Second World War, a radio transmitter was attached to a balloon and floated above the Temple - the only civilian contact with the outside world. Until 1990, the temple was part of the government Academy

of Sciences for Zoological Studies. Almost as if deliberately to defile the Buddhist faith, this holy place of worship was used as a storeroom for animal skeletons and as a laboratory of taxidermy.

By the time of Perestroika, Buddhism had once again spread to European Russia and followers were registered in Leningrad, Moscow and the Baltic states. In 1990, the Temple was returned to its believers and now has 13 monks and a new Lama. The façade is being restored and donations from Buddhist monasteries around the world have added to the collection of holy symbols needed to decorate the temple once more. Behind the scaffold on the portico still stands the once-golden Wheel of Knowledge, flanked by images of 'the gentle doe and deer, who listen to the teachings of the Master with pure hearts'.

ABOVE & LEFT:
Traditionally, the temple faces south with the main place of worship lit by an overhead glass roof. In the northern section, the most holy area, stands the altar, before which is a throne for the Lama. This temple is also a monastery, and the monks pray, meditate and have an audience with the Lama in the area between the columns.

GEOGRAPHIC INSTITUTE

Peter the Great, as befits a great adventurer, was interested in both map-making and geographical expeditions. The first national atlas made in Russia was created sometime in the 1720-30s, but the 'Golden Age' of Russian geographic studies was from 1880 up to the First World War. In this period, Dokuchaev (1846-1903) developed his theory of soil formation and natural zones and Voeykov (1842-1916) published *Climates of the World* (1884). His theories of heat and moisture balance are derived from studying conditions within Russia, in particular the 'black earth' steppe and the 'taiga' (coniferous forest). These theories eventually had considerable influence on world science.

The Imperial Russian Geographical Society was founded in 1845, and meetings were first held in the apartment of the prominent Decembrist, Pushchin, on the Moika. The first patron was Grand Duke Mikhail Nikolaevich, himself a great traveller and collector. The Geographical Society became recognized as one of the most successful learned societies in pre-Revolutionary Russia, with branches in Siberia and the Caucasus. Together with the Russian Academy of Sciences, large scale exploratory journeys were made to Central Asia, Mongolia, Northern China and Tibet; the spoils brought back from such expeditions added to the increasing collections of Eastern artefacts in the capital. Due to the mediation of the Geographical Society, Prince Kropotkin – who was incarcerated in the Peter & Paul Fortress – was able to finish his account of his expedition to Finland, which became the basis for the theories about the European Ice Age. In 1862, Alexander II assigned an apartment in the Public Education Ministry in Chernyshev Square for the society to use, and it only moved into its current home in 1909.

This building was designed specifically for the Geographical Society by the architect Gabriel V. Baranovsky. Baranovsky had been architect for the Eliseev building, and later designed the Buddhist Temple, and this building is also in the Russian Modern style. Begun in 1907, it was even equipped with telephones from the very beginning. The Religious/ Philosophical Society used the large hall for meetings – the statue of Buddha, no doubt waiting for its placement in the

LEFT: *The unusual hanging bankers' lamp is on a pulley system, so its height can be adjusted. The Geographic Council, both past and present, have met around this table.*

OVERLEAF PAGE 140: *All the original features have survived two world wars and the Revolution, including this massive stained glass window on the staircase and the delicate Modern light.*

OPPOSITE PAGE: *The Library, with its central gallery, contains many treasures. Rare books are locked up in mahogany cupboards, and busts of prominent cartographers and scientists, such as Vavilov, the plant geneticist, line the walls alongside photographs from expeditions.*

RIGHT: *The Great Hall still has the original large Modern chandelier. The room is used for lectures and talks, and the chairs have slots to take the visiting cards of guests.*

Temple, would be covered with a sheet so as not to offend the Christians. The purpose-built Library holds many treasures, including two original 19th-century globes and an ornate art deco book given to the Society to commemorate 300 years of the Romanov Dynasty in 1913. It also includes 13,000 books which once belonged to Yul Mikhailovich Shokalsky, the first President of the Physical Geographic Department, presented by his daughter after his death.

The Geographic Institute building seems to have remained remarkably untouched throughout two world wars and the Revolution. However, the international standing of the Geographical Society diminished after the Revolution, as its resources were turned inwards to serve the Soviet State. After Glasnost it was finally admitted that Soviet maps had been deliberately distorted for over 50 years to make Russia look larger – even though it already covers one sixth of the world's land mass. Political geography, which had been forbidden since 1930, also suddenly re-emerged, focusing on the ethnic communities within Russia. Despite the new openness, some official paranoia about strangers still exists – when I met the Director, he immediately phoned Paris to talk to Boris Galitzine, a distant cousin – who knows my family well – to check that I was the real thing!

THE YEARS OF REVOLUTION

IN THE YEARS LEADING UP TO the October Revolution a middle class developed, and by 1913 Russia was one of the richest countries in Europe. The arts flourished and there was a bohemian café society. However, the gulf between the wealthy and the mass populace was immense, the plight of most Russians during the First World War was disastrous and the majority of peasants were still illiterate. By 1917 the Russians were at breaking point and Lenin, with his captivating ability to make speeches promising a fairer, better world, was the catalyst that led to the destruction of Tsarist Russia. Although there were very few interiors built during the revolutionary years, this period had the greatest effect on Russian life and led to the appropriation by the State of all private property for utilitarian purposes.

After the abdication of the Tsar, the city was renamed Petrograd. Soon the rich were evicted from their houses and apartments, many of which were divided into shared housing facilities for several families known as communal flats. The aristocracy fled, taking with them anything they could carry – mainly icons, family jewels and linen – and in their absence houses were looted, furniture ruined, cellars raided and ornamentation ripped off walls.

In the early years of the Soviet state, a few grand houses were opened to the public as Museums of the City to illustrate the excesses of the rich. In them were packed the huge collections of carpets, furniture, paintings and sculpture that had been amassed by expropriating the possessions of the wealthy. Some prominent party figures moved into former mansions, changing little in their surroundings and using the luxurious furnishings, although Lenin himself was a man of simplicity.

There are over 270 locations in the city and its environs that have associations with Lenin. He spent less than six years in the area, but lived at many different addresses as he continually had to move on to avoid arrest. After his death – and up to as late as 1977 – places associated with Lenin were made into museums, the interiors preserved and recreated with help from his contemporaries. On the walls of buildings scattered throughout the city are granite plaques, giving the dates of his visit to each address. Today only a few are left, puzzling shrines to a man whose ideals have ultimately failed.

ALEXANDER BLOK'S APARTMENT

Alexander Blok (1880-1921) was the main Symbolist poet of Russia. Blok is also a fine example of the Russian intelligentsia of the time, dissatisfied with the state of Russia, yet alienated from the victorious Bolsheviks because of his upbringing. He was born into an academic family – his maternal grandfather was rector of St Petersburg University – and he grew up on the country estate of

Shakhmatovo, playing with the neighbouring family, the Mendeleevs. He later went on to marry the famous scientist's daughter, Lyubov, an actress who, as well as working with Meyerhold, gave readings of her husband's most famous work, *The Twelve* (1918).

In 1912, Blok moved into this apartment in the area known as Kolomna - Anna Pavlova lived opposite, and it was then still

ABOVE & RIGHT: *Blok's upbringing was very traditional and his taste remained so. He allowed his wife to decorate her rooms in the fashionable Modern style, but preferred to keep the furniture of his childhood around him.*

OPPOSITE PAGE: *The wallpaper in Blok's study has been copied from the original, found under many layers from the communal apartments in the building over the past decades. Most of the furniture was originally from his family estate.*

on the outskirts of the city. From around 1910 onwards Blok was famous: he would give hypnotic renditions of his work in public, 'his hair crowning his head like a halo,' as Nina Berberova, a contemporary, wrote. Yet as a person, he was shy and reticent, with a nervous disposition. He remained close to his mother throughout his life; through her work as a translator he had first been introduced to French Symbolist poetry.

Guests to Blok's apartment included Anna Akhmatova, Sergei Esenin, Mayakovsky and Meyerhold. Andrei Bely, who was hopelessly in love with Lyubov and therefore tirelessly critical of Blok, also came regularly. Blok was not a social person, so these were genuine friends, with whom creative discussions could be held. Later this period became known as the Silver Age of Russian literature.

Blok's early work was highly romantic, but he became disillusioned and cynical about the future of the human race, much to the consternation of earlier admirers. He was fatalistic about the Revolution, and eventually rejected the bourgeois Symbolists, only to find his own work scorned by the Bolsheviks. He died in his mother's apartment downstairs,

from a weak heart caused by malnutrition. The singing and shouting of drunken sailors, for whom he had been forced to move out of his home, proved too much for his delicate condition. At his funeral, crowds of people followed his coffin; Andrei Bely was a pall bearer, the bourgeoisie mingled with Red Army soldiers, ladies from salons, from theatrical and academic circles, people from all walks of life came to pay their respects and solemnly walk through the city to Smolyensky Cemetery, on the far side of Vassilievsky Island. This tradition continues today, with recitals and discussions held in the museum-flat after visiting Blok's grave, which was moved in Soviet times to Volkhovsky Cemetery.

After Blok died, Lyubov kept his possessions and on her death they were passed on to the Institute of Russian Literature. In 1980, to celebrate 100 years since Blok's birth, the apartment was designated as a museum in his memory. His death mask is on display, as well as the crown of flowers from his wedding, his favourite picture, his grandfather's desk ornament, the tray and tablecloth from Shakhmatovo – all intimate details of the poet's life.

OLD CAFÉ

St Petersburg only developed a café culture in the mid 19th century. Before this, the very rich ate banquets, either at home or as guests, and the very poor ate what they could – often going to stolovayas (public dining rooms). Incidentally, there is a famous story about Russian troops entering Paris after the Napoleonic Wars and demanding to be fed 'Bistro!' (which means 'quick' in Russian), which led to many enterprising Frenchmen opening cafés and calling them Bistros.

In St Petersburg, each era has had its legendary establishment. The Café of Wulf and Beranger was famous as the place where Pushkin met his second, Danzas, before the fatal duel with d'Anthès. Renamed the Literature Café, it relies today on this tragic event for business – it is certainly not the food that attracts the clientele. By the end of the 19th century the most famous rendezvous was Café Vienna, where Lenin met his Bolshevik comrades during 1905-6 to discuss Revolutionary politics.

On New Year's Eve, 1912, the bohemian café The Stray Dog opened. Located in a cellar near Arts Square, it held literary and artistic events, sometimes organized, sometimes spontaneous, often avant-garde. The walls were decorated with flowers and birds by artist Sergei Sudeikin and regulars included Anna Akhmatova, Vladimir Mayakovsky and Osip Mandelstam. Tamara Karsavina danced here, encircled with garlands, and next day received an almanac entitled Bouquet, hot off the press and filled with poetry from admirers of the night before. Gnedov performed his silent poetry and Ilya Sats and Arthur Lurie experimented with their 'theatre of reality', using sounds from objects to create music. The café existed until 1918 on very little money, just the energy of its guests.

In Soviet times such frivolous places were abolished, and it was only after the Second World War that new bohemians began to emerge. In the late 1950s jazz culture started to trickle into the Soviet Union, and a cafeteria on Malaya Sadovaya called Ottepel opened. Here people met to discuss creative, social and personal problems; the authorities knew of it and kept one ear open for trouble. Ottepel paved the way for the famous Saigon café in the city centre, which opened in

the 1970s. Smelling of cheap smoke and filled with young people who liked pop music, Saigon became the nucleus for 'hippie' culture in Russia. According to one regular, now a successful middle-aged businessman, 'The snacks were awful, the coffee OK, but the spirit of freedom and brotherhood kept like-minded people chatting for hours surrounding the uncomfortable stand-up tables.'

In the Capitalist CIS, there is now an Internet Café and several Art Cafés, as well as a five-star version of the Café Vienna. The unusual Old Café has remained open longer than most – probably due to its intimate atmosphere and limited table space. I feel it has captured something of St Petersburg that we all seek and have spent many an entertaining evening here, conversing excitedly against the wild piano-playing in the corner.

LEFT: *The food is traditional Russian, from pelmeni (Siberian ravioli) to bortsch (vegetable soup).*

OPPOSITE PAGE: *Above the basin in the corner is an authentic 19th-century hand washer. All the bottles and bric-à-brac are genuine antiques, collected from markets and street stalls.*

LEFT: *The decor was inspired by an early 19th century painting in the Academy of Arts. The designer, Andrei Dmitriev, deliberately left the place half finished, varnishing the bricks to hold in dust and keeping lighting low.*

ELIZAROV APARTMENT

LEFT: *Room belonging to Mark Elizarov, Lenin's brother-in-law, who housed the revolutionary for three months in 1917. Books by his favourite author, Nekrasov, can be found in the bookcase.*

BELOW: *The bedroom of Lenin's sisters, Olga and Anna. Personal belongings such as Anna's opera glasses are on display.*

A freed peasant, and one of 13 children, Mark Elizarov was married to Lenin's sister, Anna. At St Petersburg University, Mark had met Alexander Ulianov, Lenin's revolutionary brother, and was later arrested for having his telephone number. From then on he had trouble getting a good job because he had a police record. On Lenin's return to Russia from Zurich in 1917, he moved into the Elizarovs' apartment with his wife, Nadezhda Krupskaya (often known simply by her surname). Although Lenin stayed for only about three months, he was registered as living there. His registration documents state that he was the 47-year-old descendant of a courtier and Orthodox – ironic, given that he had returned to Russia to destroy these traditions, after living for ten years in

LEFT: *The bedroom of Lenin and Krupskaya. Lenin slept little and at this plain desk he managed to write 175 brochures, articles, documents and letters, and to prepare 80 speeches, during his 90-day stay. A padded easy chair that belonged to Maria Alexandrovna, his mother, stands in the room in a glass case. This chair was especially treasured by Lenin, who was abroad at the time of his mother's death in 1916.*

Europe. Of all the shrines to Lenin, this is the only one that gives any human aspect to the man. The Elizarovs had an adopted son, Gora, and a vivid story is told by the curator of how, when Lenin chased the little boy round the table, Gora broke its marble top and Lenin took the blame.

Lenin covered his room with books, and being a practical man ('my jacket hangs on a nail, Nadia's cardie hangs on the bed, but I have no place for books and papers'), he made the cupboard into a bookcase. Today the bookcase holds his cap, waistcoat and trousers, plus a beautiful pair of unworn hunter's boots – all his own personal possessions, which are kept carefully wrapped in tissue paper away from the public eye.

Relaxation was not high on Lenin's agenda at this time, although he apparently loved to read foreign dictionaries. Gorky recalls Lenin's delight at listening to a piece of Beethoven for the first time, and then his rejection of the 'escapism' it provided from 'hellish reality'. He divided his time between the Kshesinskaya Mansion and the *Pravda* printing offices, where both his sisters worked and translated for him. By July, the provisional government had marked him out as a dangerous enemy – it was at this point that he sought sanctuary at the Alliluyevs' for a couple of nights and then disappeared into a haystack on the Finnish gulf. This haystack became the first of the many Lenin Museums in 1927, but over the past ten years kept being burnt down, and now no longer exists.

RIGHT: *Original copper bathtub and water heater, kept as it was in Lenin's time.*

RIGHT: *In the main room, conferences and talks with members of the Central Committee and other leaders of the Bolshevik Party took place. The museum was furnished in 1927 with the guidance of Anna Elizarova, and many authentic household articles and pieces of furniture were used.*

After the October Revolution, Mark Elizarov and Anna continued to live in the apartment, with Olga, Lenin's other sister, and Gora. Mark died in 1919 of typhoid, having worked as the People's First Railroad Minister for a year. All the family is buried in the Volkhovsky Cemetery, except for Lenin, who famously lies embalmed in his tomb in Red Square, Moscow.

KSHESINSKAYA MANSION

If there is one house that illustrates the span of 20th-century Russia, it is the luxurious residence of the Mariinsky's prima ballerina, Mathilda Felixovna Kshesinskaya. It is located on the Petrogradsky side of the city, where there is a preponderance of Russian art nouveau, the Modern style of architecture. It was built in 1904, by Alexander Ivanovich von Gogen.

Kshesinskaya was originally from a theatrical family and trained at the Vaganova School. On her graduation in 1890, Tsar Alexander III said to her, 'Be the jewel and glory of our ballet.' In the ballerina's memoirs, written much later in Paris, she writes, 'I felt the Emperor's words as a command.' Mathilda soon met Tsarevich Nicholas and they fell in love. For a while the Tsar approved of this liaison, as it kept Nicholas off the streets where he picked up unsuitable girls, but eventually the heir to the throne had to marry a princess of his own rank. They remained friends, however, and the liaison was never forgotten — neither by those involved nor by Soviet historians. After Tsarevich Nicholas, Mathilda had many courtly admirers, including Grand Duke Sergei Mikhailovich, but a long romance with Grand Duke Andrei Vladimirovich led to the birth of her son, Vova.

Mathilda Felixovna moved from her former residence on the English Embankment to the Kshesinskaya Mansion in order to have rooms for her son. Inside, she had her own marble swimming pool, a winter garden and animals in the yard, including a cow for fresh milk every day. She also kept a goat, which had featured in her hit ballet *Esmerelda*, and was often photographed at home with this pet. Her wine cellar was renowned as one of the best in the city and dinners were sometimes given in the basement, where guests could choose their favourite wine and eat delicacies, prepared by her chef, off Limoges porcelain.

LEFT: *'Ilyich's Corner', Lenin's office in Vova's former bedroom. Lenin's desk in the foreground is in Swedish-American style, from the beginning of the 20th century, made at the Meltzer factory. The original furniture disappeared and copies were made in the experimental factory 'Intourist', again from natural materials. The rooms were reconstructed in 1987 from the descriptive notes of Podvoysky, who was a member of the Central Committee here in 1917.*

OPPOSITE PAGE: *View through the Big Marble Hall, reconstructed in 1984-7 to its former glory, with crystal and bronze chandeliers and candelabras. At the end is the winter garden.*

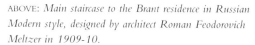

ABOVE: *Main staircase to the Brant residence in Russian Modern style, designed by architect Roman Feodorovich Meltzer in 1909-10.*

Across the enormous breadth of the Neva from the Kshesinskaya house was the former British Embassy. The daughter of the British Ambassador of the time, Meriel Buchanan, remembers how Lenin, having travelled through Germany in a sealed carriage, came to the mansion early in the spring of 1917 and filled it with his followers: 'A large red flag waved over the roof, every night lights blazed from the windows, every day crowds surged all round the house, while from a little kiosk at the corner of the garden, Lenin spoke to them, inciting them against the war, against the Government, against the Allies.' The property became the headquarters of the Bolshevik Central Committee from April to July, whilst Lenin was living with his sister, Anna Elizarova, also on Petrogradsky side. He gave famous orations from the balcony of Vova's bedroom and placed his desk and secretary in the child's quarters, as the rooms had the best light.

Kshesinskaya had received a threatening note, warning her of the Bolsheviks' intention to occupy her house. She moved out with her son and his nanny only the night before a throng of furious men raided her house and headed straight for the wine cellar. Over the next three months, moving from relatives to friends, Mathilda bravely but unsuccessfully tried to redeem her property through the Petrograd officials. She saw her house

being looted and her clothes worn by revolutionaries – in particular she recounts in her memoirs how she saw Alexandra Kolontai, leader of the Women's Movement, taking a walk round the garden wearing her ermine coat. Mathilda and Grand Duke Andrei Vladimirovich eventually emigrated to France and married in Cannes in 1921, after the death of his disapproving mother. In Paris she set up a ballet studio of some renown, with students such as Margot Fonteyn. She died in 1972, at the age of 99, never having forgotten her beloved house in St Petersburg and the Mariinsky Theatre.

The Bolsheviks' Bicycle Battalion remained in the house, gradually ruining the interior. Other societies and organizations used the building, including at the end of the 1920s an institution for mentally handicapped children. A neighbour wrote of witnessing the 'children's playful attack on a white grand piano with axes and their joyful throwing of porcelain statues against the walls'.

In 1937 the house became the Museum of S.M. Kirov, displaying documents and objects of Communist Party significance. During this time, many walls and floors were changed and the original interiors designed by Alexander Dmitriev in 1905-6 were altered or lost.

The Museum of the Great October Revolution opened in

OPPOSITE PAGE RIGHT: *Remembrance of the Future: Russia 1917 and early 1990s, an installation inviting the visitor to think about the situation today – is Russian history repeating itself and could there be a new October Revolution? In the background is a maquette of the storming of the Winter Palace, with the banner representing the Orthodox Church in the foreground.*

RIGHT: *Detail of one of the stained glass panels.*

BELOW: *Marble staircase added in 1954 to link the two residences, by architect N.N. Nadezhdin. The stained glass windows show heroes and heroines of the Great October Revolution.*

1957, created from the Kshesinskaya Mansion and the neighbouring house once owned by the bourgeois merchant, Vassily Emanuelovich Brant.   The houses were joined by a vestibule, including a basement cloakroom and stained glass windows with representations of Soviet ideology.   In 1991, the building was renamed the Government Museum of Political History. Today, it shows exhibits from each period the house has lived through, including the ballet and the wealth of Imperial Russia, plans for the Revolution, Lenin's study, an altar to Soviet power, and vitrines displaying mementoes from Perestroika – including the video camera Gorbachev used during the 1991 coup.

The Winter Garden is used for modern ballet performances and presentations and in 1992 I was privileged to be the presenter at the first 'St Petersburg Young Fashion Designers' show.   Once more chaos and excitement filled these walls. Mannequins in bizarre costumes tramped up and down the catwalk to loud music; yet another era of Russian history began its marching in this marble hall.

PRINTING MUSEUM

S t Petersburg was not quite ten years old when the first printing presses were set up to publish the first native newspaper, *The Russian Gazette*. As the majority of Russians were still illiterate, it was directed at lesser officials to keep them abreast of new reforms. The first Russian periodical, launched in 1728, was the *St Petersburg News*. By the end of the 19th century there were over 1,000 publications, of which 600 were dailies.

In 1762, Peter III passed a manifesto freeing noblemen from their obligation to serve the State. This helped to encourage some to read and others to write – Nikolai Novikov's *The Drone* being one of the most noteworthy publications. By the time of Nicholas I, the censors were hard at work and illegal printing-presses were seized, yet despite this Alexander Herzen noted in 1838: 'We have papers to represent the mining interest and the pickled herring interest, the interests of the French and the Germans, the marine interest and the land-carriage interest and all published at the expense of the Government.' Due to constant harassment from the IIIrd Department, he went on to publish the Russian literary journal *The Bell* in London; the new Tsar Alexander II was said to have been a regular reader.

Pravda (Truth) was the newspaper first established by the Bolshevik Social-Democratic party in 1912 in St Petersburg; it was the first legal Bolshevik publication. Lenin, then living in Zurich, wrote letters and articles regularly. He also kept records of subscribers and those funding its publication, to assess support for the party. After his return to Russia in April 1917, he worked daily at the paper, supervising the editorial office. His wife, Krupskaya, and sister, Anna, also worked at the paper, which was based in a flat on the Moika Embankment. On July 5, 1917, the *Pravda* offices were closed, and the newspaper was banned – the Provisional Government had recognized its strength and Lenin and other leading Bolsheviks went into hiding.

The Soviet Union inherited a variety of publications in the aftermath of the Revolution. Most were eliminated by the 1920s, leaving the two dailies: *Pravda*, now the newspaper of the Communist Party's Central Committee and *Izvestia* (News), the government paper published by the Presidium of the Supreme Soviet. Other organizations had their own journals, but major stories were all from the same source and under the control of the same censors. Nikolai Bukharin was the first editor of *Pravda* in Moscow after the Revolution, but in 1930 he was removed by his former colleague, Stalin. As a final word he printed: 'The paper with the sacred name, prints the filthiest lie, that I, Nikolai Bukharin, wish to destroy the triumphs of October, to restore capitalism'. In 1934, he was reinstated as editor of *Izvestia*. It is only over the last decade that *Pravda* and *Izvestia* have actually lived up to their names, while the market is now flooded with publications on every subject. Even glossy international magazines have offices in Moscow, and foreign periodicals are no longer hidden under hotel counters.

ABOVE: *From this office, Lenin supervised the editorial department of* Pravda *from April to July 5, 1917. He submitted 170 articles to 99 editions of the paper. In this period the paper carried a discussion page, where people could argue, discuss, make up and move forward together.*

ABOVE: *From 1865, every paper could choose which way it would be censored: before or after publication. The big newspapers paid 2,500 roubles in advance and made their own judgement on what to print. If a newspaper supported a subversive idea, it would be suspended for a while, or even closed down after three ministerial warnings.*

OPPOSITE PAGE: *The old Cyrillic alphabet had 36 letters, the modern version has 32. This printing works belonged to the* Rural Herald (Selskovo Vestnik) *from 1881 onwards. It was also used to print the pre-Revolutionary* Pravda, *and the original equipment has been on display in the Printing Museum since 1984.*

> *There is a joke about Lenin coming back to life during the Cold War, and demanding to see the issues of* Pravda *since his death. He locks himself away for weeks of reading but does not reappear, so someone is despatched to see what has happened. The* Pravdas *have obviously been thoroughly read, but Lenin is gone. Instead there is a hand-written note saying: 'You have made a mess of it. I've gone back to Zurich to start again.'*

AURORA

urora was the Roman goddess of the dawn – an appropriate name for the cruiser that fired the inaugural shot of the October Revolution, which began a new era of Russian history. At 9pm on October 25, 1917, the alarm was sounded on the ship and its crew took up battle stations. At 9.40pm a searchlight was trained on the Winter Palace from the Peter & Paul Fortress. On Commissar Belishev's command, a blank shot from the *Aurora*'s six-inch forecastle gun was fired. The storming of the Winter Palace had begun.

The *Aurora* inherited her name from one of the last 19th-century sailing ships of the Russian navy, a 44-gun frigate, distinguished in the defence of Petropavlovsk-Kamchatka in the Crimean War (1854). The new, 'Revolutionary' *Aurora* was a light, armour-plated cruiser equipped with six-inch

long-range guns, torpedo tubes and eight 37mm guns, designed to escort large battleships. Sent in 1905 to the Korean Strait with the Russian fleet, she was totally unprepared for the barrage of warships that met them at the Battle of Tsushima. *Aurora* fought heroically, but was badly damaged and trapped in Manila until peace was declared in 1906 and she returned to Kronstadt.

The bad defeat suffered in the Russo-Japanese war resulted in a full revision of the Russian navy. The fleet had been sent out poorly equipped and badly organized – mainly due to the inadequacy of Grand Duke Alexei as General Admiral of the Russian Navy. It was therefore decided that practical training must be given to naval officers, and the cruiser *Aurora* became one such training vessel.

After the outbreak of the First World War, the cruiser once again resumed military service, but in 1916 needed an overhaul. Due to a shortage of skilled workers, some of the repairs were done by the crew themselves and, as a result, they came into close contact with the revolutionary workers of Petrograd. On February 28, 1917, the sailors seized weapons and took command of the ship, supporting the insurgent shipyard workers and becoming the first naval ship to join the February Revolution.

On the night of October 24, the *Aurora* was ordered to take up position by the Nikolaevsky Bridge, which had been raised and was guarded by military cadets. When the cruiser with its

ABOVE & OVERLEAF PAGES 156 TO 157: *The* Aurora *is a floating museum staffed by 80 officers and men, who live on board. The bugle still sounds, the sailors' uniforms are immaculate and every day the flags are raised and lowered, but this hulk of grey metal, which once represented so much pride, now seems just a reminder of failed Revolutionary dreams.*

powerful guns arrived, the cadets fled; the ship's electricians lowered the bridge and detachments of armed workers and revolutionary military units were able to march towards Palace Square. On October 25, the *Aurora*'s radio station transmitted Lenin's manifesto 'To the Citizens of Russia', announcing the overthrow of the Provisional Government. That evening, the shot fired by the guns had changed the course of the 20th century.

RIGHT: *The* Aurora's *engine room, which is spotless as the ship never moves from this position. The celebration of the beginning of the October Revolution is now held on November 7, because after the Julian calendar of the Orthodox church was changed on May 1, 1917 to the Gregorian, all dates moved 13 days on from pre-Revolutionary times.*

OPPOSITE PAGE: *The original cruiser* Aurora *was deliberately sunk somewhere between Oranienbaum and Kronstadt, in order to protect it from ceaseless bombing in the Second World War. In 1948 the cruiser was raised and moored opposite the Nakhimov Naval School. It is now a replica due to the deterioration of the original craft.*

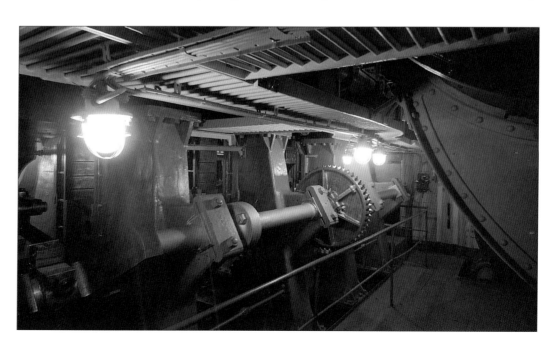

ALEXANDER PALACE

The Alexander Palace was built at Tsarskoe Selo in 1792, to celebrate the marriage of Catherine the Great's favourite grandson, Alexander. Some consider it to be Quarenghi's greatest work, and certainly the strict Classicism of the building is in sharp contrast to its Baroque neighbour, the ornate Catherine Palace – which Alexander I preferred. His brother, Nicholas I, spent more time in the new palace than the intended owner, as did Alexander III, but the Romanovs who made it their own were the last Imperial couple.

Nicholas and Alexandra remained in almost perpetual seclusion at Tsarskoe Selo – so much so that by 1912 the Tsar had spent only one night in St Petersburg since his accession, and after 1905 the Empress only made day visits. In 1917, the family was placed under house arrest in this palace by the provisional government, after Nicholas had conceded to abdication. They were taken from here and eventually met their death in Ekaterinburg, where they were shot in July 1918.

After the family had left the Alexander Palace, the general public was allowed in. Red Army soldiers were on guard, ropes were placed to protect carpets and people came in droves to snoop on the private life that had been kept so secret during Nicholas' reign. The last Tsar had remained aloof from his people for several reasons; he was naturally a timid man and his German (but English-bred) wife, Alexandra, suffered red flushes of nervousness in public. They preferred the privacy of their family, the four beautiful daughters and Alexei, the haemophiliac Tsarevich, to attending official functions. Alexandra's original roots made things worse when the First

LEFT: *Since 1949 the Alexander Palace has been closed to the public, but in 1997 the East Wing was given back to the Museum of Tsarskoe Selo. The study of Nicholas II was recently restored for a Russian feature film of the last Tsar's life. The gallery led to Alexandra's suite of rooms across the corridor.*

LEFT: *Nicholas II's desk, where he worked under the watchful eye of his domineering wife. The other major influence on the weak Tsar had been his father, Alexander III, who is shown in the portrait behind the desk.*

BELOW: *In the White Reception Room, the poignant portraits of Nicholas and Alexandra remind one of their tragic lives. Ironically, they also lived with this portrait of Marie-Antoinette, who had shared a similar fate a century before. The carpet is the original; it had been kept in a basement storage room at the Hermitage.*

BELOW: *The rooms of Nicholas and Alexandra were well-documented in photographs, so the curators had excellent reference material to work from when rebuilding the interiors. This room was once filled daily with generals, ambassadors and courtiers, all waiting for an audience with the Tsar.*

World War broke out and tremendous hostility was felt towards Germans; this added to her reluctance to appear in public. It was in her suite of lilac rooms in the Alexander Palace that the notorious Rasputin would be received for tea, before working his healing magic – now thought to be hypnotism – on her beloved 'Baby', the young Tsarevich.

The palace had been closed to the public since 1949, when it was given over to a top-secret naval base. The beautiful colonnade was visible through the trees on visits to Tsarskoe Selo, and always held an air of intrigue and mystery for me – the two biggest secrets of Russia and the Soviet Union together (the murdered Tsar and military technology). Then, in 1997, a Russian film crew was allowed to recreate the interior of the East Wing for a film about the last days of the Tsar. The home of Nicholas and Alexandra was opened to the public once more, the first museum since the 1920s to show the domestic life of the last Tsar of all the Russias.

DOM OFFICERS

LEFT: *Dining room with portraits of the two Russian Generalissimos, Suvorov and Kutuzov.*

lthough each regiment had its own club, Dom Officers was a meeting place for officers from all regiments of the army and navy. It was built in 1893 by the architect Victor Ivanov, with the help of architects von Gogen, Donchenko and Gauger – a specialist in ventilation! In Soviet days, the building continued to function as a house for officers in the army, navy, airforce and police. The ballroom has been converted into a theatre, where private performances are held regularly for officers and veterans of the war.

Before the Revolution, my grandfather, Prince Vladimir Galitzine, was an officer in the Chevalier Guards. As he was tall enough, he was appointed to the squadron of Maria Feodorovna, the Dowager Empress. In his unpublished memoirs, he recalls his strict supervisor making him practise different

LEFT & OPPOSITE PAGE: *The white marble double-vaulted staircase and the extent of the reception rooms show that this was a place used to accommodate large groups of people. The Classical sculptures that decorated the pedestals on the stairs were transformed with the face of Lenin – a large white statue of the demi-god still stands illuminated on the third floor.*

gymnastic exercises in the private gym in the basement of the Officers' Club.

'Without education, without knowledge, it is not possible to be an officer,' said General Krasnov. When my grandfather left Moscow University in 1907, he came to St Petersburg to carry out his long-standing desire to join the Chevalier Guard regiment. He was accepted as a volunteer and within a year became a cornet. There is a popular song about Cornet Obolensky and Paruchik (Lieutenant) Galitzine, that reminisces about better days before Soviet times, and people often hum it in my presence. It could well have been written about my grandfather and his great friend Alexei Obolensky, both of whom served in the same regiment.

Once in the regiment regulations were strict, and after his exams Vladimir was two marks below the level needed to become an officer. Family pressure on Grand Duke Konstantine Konstantinovich, head inspector of military educational establishments, resulted in one further mark – but he was still one mark short. Promotions took place at the parade of July 22, nameday of the regiment's Commander-in-Chief, Empress Maria, and my grandfather went on parade in Peterhof, just in case. Vladimir hoped that he would be noticed and put up for promotion by Grand Duke Nicholas Nikolaevich, Commander-in-Chief of the Imperial Army, who knew him from childhood, but no such luck. The Grand Duke pretended not to see him, and he returned home without his officers' epaulettes.

Eventually my grandfather got his extra mark and became a lieutenant. The Commander of the regiment at the time was Prince Felix Yusupov, later famous for the murder of Rasputin, who apparently liked to attend manoeuvres in his motor car! When war broke out in 1914, my grandparents went to Yakshino, his maternal family estate. Nearby borzoi trials were taking place, and Grand Duke Nicholas was present. He

LEFT: *The Ladies' Drawing Room, to which they could retire and rearrange their attire whilst discussing the antics of the officers next door.*

instructed his Adjutant General to invite Lt. Prince Galitzine to become his aide-de-camp. Indirectly, through this promotion, my family escaped revolutionary Russia – in 1915, the Tsar took over Supreme Command of the Russian Army, and Grand Duke Nicholas was sent as Viceroy to the Caucasus, taking my grandfather with him. From there, my grandparents and their three small sons were able to escape on a British ship, HMS *Grafton*, across the Black Sea and through to Europe, where they found sanctuary in England in 1919.

A little-known fact is that on January 5, 1918, from the Officers' Club roof, Bolshevik soldiers fired at oncoming demonstrators marching from the Field of Mars to protest at Lenin surrounding the Tauride Palace with troops for the opening of the Constituent Assembly. It was the first time since Bloody Sunday in 1905 that unarmed people had been fired upon by their own, and thirty people were killed. For scholars, this date marks the beginning of the armed suppression of the people. In January 1998 there was a memorial service and demonstration held in front of the Officers' Club in memory of this tragic event but only 80 people came, since so few people know the truth of what really happened under Lenin's regime.

ABOVE & RIGHT: *This suite of rooms leads off the Tsar's private room. There was a special entrance for the Tsar, with an elevator taking him directly to his reception room. His Imperial Highness would receive commended officers, before attending a banquet or ball on the premises. Surrounding his room is a balcony, from which he would appear to the general public.*

SMOLNY INSTITUTE

ABOVE: *The room where Lenin lived was kept like a shrine during the Soviet period, showing the monastic style in which he lived with his wife, Nadezhda Krupskaya.*

LEFT: *From October 25, 1917, to March the following year, this was Lenin's office. The brass plaque with the words 'Classnaya Dama' (Class Matron) remains on the door just as he left it.*

In 1764, Catherine the Great – the 'enlightened despot' – decided to educate the daughters of Russian gentry. On May 5 the Imperial Educational Association for Noble Ladies was begun; it was the first educational institution for girls, and only for those of noble birth. The girls were sent to school at five or six years old and spent 12 years there, meeting their parents only on Thursdays or Sundays under the strict supervision of their governess.

Maria Feodorovna, wife of Paul I, took a great interest in the school and in 1806 Giacomo Quarenghi was commissioned to design a special building for the Smolny Institute. Prior to this, it had been housed next door, attached to Rastrelli's baroque Smolny Convent. The area was known as Smolyanoy dvor after the 'tar yards' of Peter the Great's shipbuilding time. Quarenghi's design is heavily influenced by English Palladian; the building is pale yellow with white columns and Classical features.

'Smolyankas', as the girls were known, were educated to serve in the Imperial Court as ladies-in-waiting or as suitable wives for nobles. Alexander II fell in love with his famous mistress, Katya Dolgorukaya, when she was still a Smolyanka. There were three separate classes: brown, blue and white. The girls learnt cooking, sewing, ironing and handicrafts along with a highly academic curriculum. Later, Alexander II introduced sciences and history as subjects. Lessons were taken in French – when three surviving Smolyankas recently visited the White Hall they immediately began to converse in French.

The Institute, financed by the Imperial Court, existed until March 1917, when the girls went away for Easter, never to return. After the February Revolution, no more funding for the

school was available and in August the buildings became the Party Headquarters when the Central Executive Committee and the Petrograd Soviets moved there from the Tauride Palace. Lenin came on the evening of October 24, and it was from the White Hall - which became known as the Assembly Hall – that on the following day the Second All-Russian Congress of Soviets claimed Communist power, with Lenin shouting out his first decrees for peace and for land.

After the Central Committee moved to Moscow in 1918, the Smolny became the Party Headquarters for Leningrad and surrounding provinces. It was in these halls that Leonid Nikolaev assassinated the local Party boss, Sergei Kirov. Stalin came to Leningrad to interrogate him personally. In 1923-4 two Classical propylaea were built with the slogans 'Workers of

ABOVE: *Quarenghi's original White Hall is divided into three sections by two rows of Classical columns. Here the dance classes were taught and, on special occasions, balls were held, to which young boys from privileged military academies and the Emperor's Court were invited.*

OVERLEAF PAGE 166: *Inside are long, wide corridors with many doors leading to the dormitories or classrooms. When Trotsky lived here, he threatened to bring his bicycle to travel from room to room.*

All Countries Unite' and 'The First Soviet of the Proletarian Dictatorship' written in the porticoes above busts of Marx and Engels. During the war the Smolny was covered in camouflage nets, which would be changed according to the season. The deep two-storey basement became a bomb shelter and food storage depot for the workers. The Smolny is now used as the offices of the City Governor.

STALIN AND THE
SECOND WORLD WAR

I N 1927, THREE YEARS AFTER THE DEATH OF LENIN, Petrograd was renamed Leningrad. Streets were also renamed, either in memory of Lenin or to encourage the workers – for instance Tractor Street, which was created in 1925 to commemorate the first tractors manufactured in the Soviet Union. During Stalin's rule, the buildings of the city were subjected to a series of assaults. Many places of worship were desecrated and transformed to fulfil other functions: the Church of the Nativity became an ice rink; the St Peter & Paul Lutheran Church an Olympic-size swimming pool; the Orthodox Cathedral of St Andrew on Vassilievsky Island was converted into an anthropological workshop, with rows of skulls lined up across the iconostasis. Former palaces and private mansions were also modified for use by the State.

Stalin issued a decree moving the bulk of the population into cities, so a great deal of construction work was launched in the suburbs. Factories were also built, with associated workers' housing. The Classical style of architecture was used: not only was this emotionally powerful and huge in scale, but most qualified architects had been trained in the Neo-classical style before the Revolution. Stalinesque Classicism dominates Moscow, and in Leningrad housed Party members and the privileged. These buildings are very sturdy and are still thought of as prestigious dwellings. Soviet authorities did not even consider trying to recoup the huge investment in housing through rents, which have remained at the 1928 level.

The Second World War interrupted the ambitious construction programmes of the 1930s, and in 1941 the Nazis destroyed five and a half million sqm of housing. Although the population of the city was been tragically diminished during the Siege of Leningrad, plans to rebuild the city were begun immediately. After 1945, huge restoration projects also commenced, and most of the summer palaces, the Anichkov Palace and Nevsky Prospekt were almost restored to their former glory by the 1950s.

ALLILUYEV APARTMENT

As I investigate the lesser-known palaces and mansions in St Petersburg, there is an eerie feeling of something left unexplained. So many ornate cornices in grand halls were left unharmed, so many imperial palaces became museums, and yet so few of the 'people's' lives were preserved with the same respect. Yet the Communist Party's intention was not to glorify the lives of the wealthy, but to expose them as mindless spendthrifts, living in excess while peasants starved outside. Then one stumbles upon the little-known apartment of Jacob Alliluyev, father of Nadezhda, the second wife of Stalin. Jacob, his wife and their four children lived here from March 1917 until they moved to the new capital, Moscow, in 1918 with their powerful friends, Lenin and Stalin. Here is a perfect example of an ordinary family home,

ABOVE: *An artist's rendition mocking the cult of Communism. Busts of Lenin belonging to the museum are placed on columns of his tomes, 55 volumes published in every language.*

OPPOSITE PAGE: *The main room – the parents sacrificed their bedroom for the political guests and made do with sleeping in the living room. A third room was kept for the daughters, but was occupied by Zinoviev and his wife when the children were away. Photographs on the walls show members of the family.*

TOP RIGHT: *Room allocated by the Alliluyev family to Joseph Stalin, from where he went to work at Smolny in 1917. Lenin stayed here for three days in July 1917. Zinoviev and Ordzhonikidze no doubt slept on the divan after a long night of discussion.*

before being smuggled away to the haystack near the Gulf of Finland. It was in this home that Stalin first saw his future wife, Nadezhda, a keen piano player and only 16, fresh from the gymnasium. One room was specially allocated to Stalin – he and Jacob had known one another in the Caucasus – but he chose to use it only after Lenin's visit.

The museum was created in 1938, an affiliation of the Lenin Museum, simply because Lenin stayed here for three days. The differences between the biographical details of Lenin's life and Stalin's are astonishing. Lenin's every memo is noted down: where he was at every minute from 1917 up to his death in 1924, filling ten volumes. In contrast, Stalin's biographical history has been carefully edited to a mere six pages of image-making events, beginning in the Caucasus and finishing in Moscow.

Two years prior to the museum's opening, Zinoviev had been shot and all mention of him removed from Soviet history, either by tampering with photographs or the omission of his name. Stalin was not sentimental towards the Alliluyev family either. Nadezhda shot herself in 1932, her brother Pavel (who supposedly provided the gun) was arrested some years later and died of a sudden 'unexpected' heart attack, and her sister Anna was arrested and released from prison only after Stalin's death. The second brother, Feodor, was an invalid after the First World War, so presumably he was judged to be harmless. The museum was opened under the vigilant eye of Stalin, checking that not too much of his private life was revealed. The Alliluyev family helped with placing furniture and providing items of interest and these are the exhibits that remain on display today.

rented by a professional from an advertisement in the newspaper.

The powerful Communist cult censored history, and has omitted to tell us that in this apartment Lenin, Zinoviev and Stalin (plus other powerful figures in the Party) plotted how to escape arrest in August 1917. Here, with Jacob's razor, Lenin shaved off his beard and donned a wig to escape recognition,

KIROV'S APARTMENT

M any streets, institutes and theatres in Leningrad were renamed in memory of the city's popular Party Secretary, Kirov, who was assassinated in 1934. If there was one Communist leader who remained uncorrupted by power, the Soviet party led the people to believe it was Sergei Mironovich Kirov. Born in Vyatka in 1886 and brought up in an orphanage, he became a committed revolutionary whilst studying in Kazan. During his life, he was imprisoned as a revolutionary in Tsarist times, was a Soviet delegate in Poland to negotiate for peace in 1920, became the RSFSR representative in Georgia and was the first Party Secretary in Azerbaijan. From 1926 he headed the Leningrad Regional Party committee. Our 'Mironovich', as he was called, was a good speaker and a good listener and was not afraid to work alongside the people, supervising polar expeditions and mining in the Urals.

After the Bolshevik take-over, the best apartments were

RIGHT: *In the library, Kirov had 20,000 volumes and gramophone records of all Lenin's speeches. He gave his duplicate books to the Putilovsky Factory. Until 1955, Kirov's possessions were on display in the Kshesinskaya Mansion, since his widow and sister continued to live in the flat after his death.*

BOTTOM RIGHT: *Although there is a rather grand study, in the evenings and at night Kirov liked to work at this dining room table, with silver carp and goldfish surrounding him in aquariums.*

given to the city's Party and industrial officials. Several large buildings had been erected on Kamennoostrovsky Prospekt prior to the Revolution – including No. 26/28, built by Leonti, Alexander and Yuli Benois in 1911 by order of the First Russian Insurance Society. A huge building with purpose-built apartments for wealthy professionals, it was considered the finest residential block of its time. It faced onto three streets, with eight inner courtyards, and a colonnade of red granite to the main entrance. Kirov lived in Apartment 20 from 1926 to the day of his assassination on December 1, 1934.

The official story on Kirov's assassination was that a young Communist, Leonid Nikolaev, wanted revenge after being sacked from the Party for White Guard sympathies. Stalin visited Leningrad to interrogate Nikolaev personally. With his death warrant, and those of 37 other party members, began the terrible purges of the 1930s. Kirov was thought of as Stalin's heir apparent and is quoted as having described the despot as 'the greatest man of all times and all peoples'. However, in the secret speech made by Khrushchev in 1956, it was implied that Stalin had instructed the Cheka to carry out the assassination. There is no doubt that Stalin felt some jealousy towards the Leningrad Party boss, as in Moscow that year there had been a vote of popularity in the Central Committee, the results of which were:

Against Kirov – 4   Against Stalin – 298

It is now generally accepted that Stalin disposed of his rival, although the curators of the memorial still deny it. The apartment is full of Kirov's possessions, including many stuffed birds and hunting mementoes as he was a keen huntsman. There is a library, dining room, study, and a little parlour – plus six other rooms that presumably the humble Kirov had no use for, as the apartment is supposed to be preserved 'just as it was when he lived here'. They are now used for exhibits.

KIROV FACTORY

The Kirov Factory was once the pride of Leningrad, the largest industrial enterprise in the whole of Russia. Over 42,000 workers produced 2000 tractors a month, as well as the tanks that equipped the 'invincible' Soviet army. At 7am and 4pm (the beginning of the two work shifts) thousands of workers would pour out of the specially-built metro station alongside the plant. As in Disneyland, special Kirovsky carts serviced the area, taking people to the various buildings. In the Cold War years the labour of a factory worker was better rewarded than that of an intellectual or a scientist, and they had a privileged allocation of theatre tickets, holiday resorts, sanatoriums and health care.

Since Perestroika the Kirovsky workforce has diminished to a mere 12,000 barely seen, yet still proud, employees. The 200km of rails that once circumnavigated the territory are overgrown with weeds and wagons stand obsolete, covered in heavy coats of congealed oil. Broken panes of glass let in the weather and there are missing light bulbs in lamps that are switched off in the lunch break to save electricity. The trappings of the worker's Utopia are still visible; huge clocks hang still and silent amongst static machinery, images from Orwell. Giant noticeboards, with space for the photographs of excellent workers, stand empty. This prime example of Soviet efficiency, the bringing together of nuts and bolts from all parts of the Soviet Union, now sits gathering dust and occasionally producing 50-100 rather forlorn yellow tractors a month.

A factory was founded on this land in 1801, in the time of Paul I, employing 400 workers to make small boats and cast

LEFT: *The factory no longer concentrates on tanks and turbines, but also makes armoured cars and ecologically safe city buses, as well as yellow tractors.*

OPPOSITE PAGE: *During the Cold War years a picture such as this would be classed as industrial espionage.*

iron cannons. The Russian industrial era began in the 1860s, and by 1873 – under the new name of the owner, Nikolai Ivanovich Putilov – the workforce had increased tenfold and the factory was producing strong, iron railway tracks of a high European quality, as good as those from England or Belgium. In 1894 the factory produced its first steam engine and by the beginning of the 20th century it was manufacturing three-mile field cannons and mine cruisers.

The factory also played an important part in the beginning of the Revolution. In late 1904, four workers at the Putilov Ironworks were dismissed for belonging to the non-political 'Assembly of Russian Factory Workers'. This 'trade union' was begun by a local priest, Father Gapon, with the approval of V.K. Pleve, the Minister of the Interior, in the very

Christian hope of gaining human rights for workers, including an eight-hour day and equal pay for women. The factory workers rose up in protest against the unfair treatment of their fellow Putilovsky workers in January 1905. This began a chain of strikes amongst metal workers in the main factories of St Petersburg, which eventually led to demonstrations in the city and the deaths of citizens on Bloody Sunday.

The plant continued to be a boiling point for revolutionary action and Lenin took advantage of this, visiting the factory several times and making speeches to encourage the workers to unite. In 1922 the factory was renamed 'Red Putilovets' and three years later, to mark its 125-year anniversary, received the Order of Red Labour. In 1934 the factory took the name of the recently murdered local hero, Kirov, and received the Order

OPPOSITE PAGE:
Apparatus made by Wohlenberg, Cincinnati, Siemelkamp, Hoesch and other industrial giants stands still and silent on the work floor.

RIGHT & BELOW:
The plant's major income is now generated by steel production and in 1997 profits totalled $32 million, with exports to over 20 countries.

of Lenin. All of these awards, in large metal casts, are pinned to the boundary walls, as though to a man's breast; every worker had the right to feel he had deserved such a merit.

During the Second World War the factory was an obvious target for Nazi bombardment. Despite this, production never stopped during the Blockade – even though workers sometimes had to tie themselves to their workspace to avoid collapsing from hunger. In the Cold War years, any connection with a foreigner was seen as industrial espionage and a photographer would certainly not have been allowed to take pictures in the plant.

The huge territory of 184 hectares, contained within tight security walls, now has the feeling of a ghost town. Apparatus made by Wohlenberg, Cincinnati, Siemelkamp, Hoesch and other industrial giants can still be found on the work floor, but it was bought in better days. Even though Yeltsin stood on a Kirovsky T-80 tank in the 1991 coup, the factory has completely changed its structure since the fall of Communism. The plant's major income is now generated by steel production, while the new need for armoured cars and ecologically safe city buses has taken the place of tank and turbine production.

Small in comparison to turnover during Communist times, profits in 1997 totalled $32 million, with exports to over 20 countries. The crane driver (always a woman and highly respected) still sits in her exalted position, shifting heavy metal up and down the warehouse, but there are no longer workers running around like ants 30m beneath her. A tank stands on a pedestal, hidden among the trees in the grounds, together with three unremoved statues of Lenin. All these are reminders of the factory's former Soviet glory, lost in the wave of privatization.

MUSEUM OF THE ARCTIC AND ANTARCTICA

The Museum of the Arctic and Antarctica, based in the former Church of St Nicholas the Miracle Worker, is currently the centre of many an argument between those who are still proud of the achievements of the Soviet Union and those who wish to revive the Church in Russia. This is not the first time that arguments have raged around this building, since it was built in the 1820s for the Orthodox Old Believers, who were continually squabbling with the Synod.

The original church, by architect Abraham Ivanovich Melnikov (1784–1854), was paid for by the merchant, Cosmo Zakharovich Chursinov. The famous street on which it stands,

Ulitsa Marata, was formerly named Nikolaevskaya after the church, which stood at the crossroads in the middle. In the time of Nicholas I it was a very important Church of Unification, despite having a small congregation of only 1000 souls. When it was closed in 1931, the NKVD found holy treasures bricked into the walls and all the priests and regular worshippers were arrested and sent to camps.

Many churches in Leningrad were destroyed, but the Church of St Nicholas was reconstructed to serve a more utilitarian purpose. In 1934 it was modernized to create the unique Museum of the Arctic and Antarctica, opened in 1937. The

centre of the church had an unusual upper gallery – originally for the choir – with a colonnade that supported the round cylinder of the roof. The building was divided at this point to create a new first floor and, because of the original perfect proportions, the upper part now seems quite natural as a separate hall. Inside the museum are original polar expedition tents, although the portrait of Lenin that once hung on the canvas wall above the camp bed has now been removed. A skip-plane that Soviet researchers used in the 1930s to investigate the Arctic hangs from the ceiling in the entrance – somewhat incongruous with the rosette carvings decorating the arch, remnants of the former church interior.

A federal decree passed in 1996 demanded the building back for the Church and now a fight is going on over its ownership. The Arctic and Antarctica Institution, whose Union Headquarters were once in the Sheremetev Palace, cannot afford to move all the exhibits to another location, which would probably be further out of town and attract even fewer visitors than today. The sad state of the museum is illustrative of the current lack of government funding in all the sciences. Russia is losing its power both in space and in the polar regions – in Antarctica last year, Australia had to assist the Mirny 'Peace' station with their fuel supplies.

ABOVE: *Recreation of the original 'Domik', the first expedition house on a drifting ice floe at the North Pole, used at the end of the 1950s and early 60s, and known as PVS/4A. The fur sleeping bag on the camp bed is made of dog's hair.*

BELOW: *Displays include the fauna of the Arctic and Antarctica, such as a stuffed polar bear, as well as heroic pictures of explorers and maps of their routes.*

ABOVE: *Glass vitrines full of penguins and seals, with their adorable chicks and cubs.*

OPPOSITE PAGE: *The first floor of the museum, with the colonnade that supports the round cylinder of the roof. Originally this was an upper gallery for the choir in the centre of the church, and the building was open from ground floor through to the roof.*

ARTILLERY MUSEUM

The impressive stronghold that is now the Artillery Museum was once the Tsar's Arsenal. Situated beyond the northern moat of the Peter & Paul Fortress, on the site of the defensive wall known as the Kronverk, the Artillery Arsenal was built in the 1850s by P.I. Tamansky in the style of a mediaeval castle. Before 1918, there was an atelier here for repairs to personal arms, and two halls exhibited the range of weapons used in battle. Now the Arsenal is guarded by disused guns and tanks. In the winter snow, these brooding machines are dramatic against the red walls.

Inside, huge, vaulted halls house a fearsome collection of exhibits, beginning with the lances, pikes and spears of Peter the Great's time, the first heavy metal guns and mortar bombs, and the miniature cannon presented to Peter by his father, when he was a child. The history of Russia is told through its weaponry: original Putilov cannon balls, a collection of duelling pistols, medals, standards for leading regiments into

battle, and portraits of the famous generals of Russia — Orlov and Potemkin, from Catherine the Great's time, and Field Marshal Kutuzov and Barclay de Tolly from the Napoleonic Wars. The largest exhibit in this hall is a ridiculously ornate carriage which belonged to Catherine the Great, from which General Suvorov addressed his troops at the Battle of Borodino.

Beyond the Romanov exhibits are halls dedicated to the Revolution, the Red Army (1918-41), the Second World War, the Defence of Leningrad and the post-war Soviet Army. It is a real 'boys' own' museum that has yet to be updated by the new Democratic Russia. Only 5% of the exhibits are on display, the rest are in storage. One of the more curious things one can see is Lenin's armoured car, moved from its pedestal outside the Marble Palace - where it has been replaced by Paul Trubetskoy's monument to Alexander III, nicknamed 'the Hippo'. In the communications section is a stuffed dog with a radar attached to his stomach; the dog would have been sent through enemy lines. Strange modelled maps of battlefields have hidden tanks and mines when one looks closer at them, and a 1930s photomontage by the German D. Harfield, 'I'm for Me!', shows the USA handing Hitler $1million. A perfect maquette of the burnt-out Reichstag on the Belorussian front even shows the Russian graffiti left on the walls.

Nowhere is it mentioned that, in 1917, sailors stormed the Arsenal and stole arms, and that this was the main source of weapons for the Revolution. It was once a fashionable status symbol to display large collections of trophies, swords and pistols on the walls; the Artillery Museum leaves one in no doubt of the strength of Soviet military power. It is only the ropes cordoning off areas that are unsafe due to lack of repairs that remind one of the reality of the Russian state today.

ABOVE: *Ramps were built into the grand staircase in Soviet times for trundling cannons up and down – pre-Revolutionary photographs show the sweeping staircase covered in plants and banners. The paintings show the storming of the Winter Palace and the victory parade in Red Square – it rained on Victory Day in Moscow 1945.*

ABOVE: *Primitive weapons remind one of the difficulties of going into battle in those times.*

RIGHT: *Some galleries hold such huge, terrifying contraptions, one wonders how they managed to get into the museum. Recently a special exhibition devoted to the Kalashnikov attracted a lot of attention from visitors arriving in dark Mercedes.*

OPPOSITE PAGE: *To enter the museum, one passes through a barrage of tanks, rockets, cannons and other heavy artillery parked in the courtyard.*

RUMIANTSEV PALACE

The Museum of the Blockade of Leningrad is now housed in the Rumiantsev Palace. During the Second World War, the city was blockaded by the Nazis for almost 900 days from September 1941 to January 1944. Although the official death toll was 640,000, it is now thought that over one million people died. According to a secret directive from Nazi naval headquarters, 'The Führer has decided to wipe the city of Petersburg off the face of the earth ... level it to the ground by shelling and continuous bombing.' No aid was sent from Moscow – perhaps because Leningrad's martyrdom was being exploited by Stalin to encourage sympathy from the allies for the Russian war effort.

In December 1941, the city's electricity supply was failing, and by January there was no household water; people lived in darkness, literally freezing to death. The bread ration was just 250g per person per day. Soups were made by boiling water and petroleum jelly; even a roast rat was not a good meal, as rats went hungry too. There were rumours of cannibalism – such meat-eaters had flushed, red faces and a wild look in their eyes. The stories of librarians refusing to burn one book at the Library, or scientists at the Vavilov Institute of Plant-Breeding not eating one exhibit of grain, illustrate the heroism and

LEFT: *Stepanov replaced the main three-joint, metal staircase with this elegant, perfectly proportioned, two-tier marble one. To achieve it, he had to break through the wall and build a new semi-circular wall with a door to the adjoining Winter Garden.*

LEFT: *The oak staircase was added in 1882-4, when the palace was owned by Duke Evgeny Leichtenburg and his wife, Zinaida. It was designed by the young architect Alexander Stepanov, whose work can also be seen in the Yusupov Palace on the Moika.*

The Rumiantsev Palace was adapted in 1824 by architect V. Glinka for Nikolai Rumiantsev, second son of Catherine the Great's favourite Peter Rumiantsev. Nikolai was an important foreign minister during the reign of Alexander I, working in close association with France. When Napoleon invaded, Rumiantsev was shocked into an apoplectic stroke, which left him partially deaf. Shortly afterwards he retired to write Russian diplomatic history. Rumiantsev financed an expedition around the world in the ship Rurik, which discovered the Rumiantsev Islands, Romanov Islands and Romanov's Ridge for Russia. He died in 1826, in the suite of rooms facing the English Embankment. He had intended the building to be a museum after his death and five years later it opened, but in 1861 – due to financial problems – it was moved to the Pashkov House in Moscow and the palace returned to private ownership. In 1918 Lunacharsky issued a law to establish 'Museums of the City' in Petrograd. Initially situated in the Anichkov Palace, the main Museum of Old Petersburg was moved to the Rumiantsev Palace in 1938.

pride of the city. Most men had been called to the Front, so the city was defended by the elderly, women and children. Twelve-year-olds worked in factories, whilst old women broke the ice to draw buckets of water from broken pipes.

Hope was kept alive by 'The Road of Life', a 37km route across the southern part of frozen Lake Ladoga. From November 1941 until April 1942, trucks trundled across the thin ice bringing in supplies, mainly sacks of flour, which increased rations by 100g per person. Cabbages were planted in the main squares, and provisions accumulated ready for the next winter. When the Blockade was finally broken in January 1944, there was rejoicing on the streets. The city itself was left half-ruined; almost every street had suffered shell damage. Monuments had been protected, buildings camouflaged, barrage balloons hung in skies to stop low-flying planes, yet still the continual bombardment from the surrounding Nazis had taken its toll. The worst damage was done in the occupied regions: Peterhof, Tsarskoe Selo, Pavlovsk and Gatchina. Departing troops burned everything in sight and left booby traps. Had Leningrad been occupied, it would have shared this fate – it was saved by its citizens' bravery and determination.

The museum holds many reminders of the horrors of the Siege. Here one can see the size of the meagre ration of bread and the diary of eleven-year-old Tanya Savicheva, who lost her family to starvation, one by one. Billboards, encouraging citizens to take care of their appearance, are displayed next to horrific pictures of skeletal people dragging corpses on sleds. During the war, the building was a shelter for museum staff and those who had lost their homes. Beds filled the halls and several families lived in each room. The restoration of the building began in 1946, and has now continued for over 50 years.

RIGHT: *Re-creation of a Leningrad flat during the Siege. It was so cold, people just sat huddled in blankets in front of temporary fires. By spring 1942, women and children were being evacuated via 'The Road of Life', but still many died each day. Bodies were left unburied and, as the snow melted, corpses rotted on the streets. Mass graves were dug and infection was rife, yet those who survived remember a feeling of euphoria – no doubt from hunger – a unifying feeling of saving their beloved city from the Fascists.*

AMBER ROOM

The Greeks believed that amber was the rays of the sun, petrified. Imagine an entire room covered with panels of amber, glowing and catching the light – no wonder the Amber Room at Tsarskoe Selo was considered to be the Eighth Wonder of the World. King Friedrich Wilhem I of Prussia presented the room as a diplomatic gift to Peter the Great in 1717, after Peter had admired it while a guest in Charlottenburg, Berlin. The room was first installed in the Winter Palace, but in 1755, Empress Elizabeth ordered Francesco Rastrelli to move it to the Catherine Palace. The individual amber panels were carried from St Petersburg to Tsarskoe Selo by 76 guardsmen in six days. They were not large enough to complete the new 100sqm decor, so mosaic and mirror insets were added and the upper part of the walls was painted to imitate amber.

During the Second World War, Nazi troops occupied the environs of Leningrad, camping in Tsarskoe Selo, Pavlovsk, Gatchina and Peterhof. The Catherine Palace was used as a stable and cowshed, with a garage for motorcycles in the church. Although the Soviet authorities evacuated most of the treasures from the palaces and sent them east as the Nazis approached, there was no time to pack up the heavy panels from the Amber Room. Occupying troops removed them in September 1941, and they were brought to Alfred Rode, head of the Konigsberg Art Museum in Kaliningrad. Part of the Amber Room was last seen on display in Konigsberg Castle, before being hidden in its catacombs. From here the mystery starts. There are stories that the amber was burnt in a bomb attack; that it was moved to Germany on the personal order of Hitler himself; that it remains in the subterranean vaults of the castle, which stretch for kilometres. The most recent and hopeful theory is that, whilst being transported to Germany, the panels were dumped in a coal mine on the Baltic Coast. The legend of the lost Amber Room has inspired films, thrillers and treasure hunters. Valued today at over $142m, it would be no small find.

Meanwhile, a team of restorers has worked since 1982 in an outhouse of the Catherine Palace, intent on recreating the magnificent room. First the design is traced from drawings and black and white photographs of the room; then a fine plasticine model is made, from which a cast in plaster is taken. This is laid out on a wood board the exact size of the panel, and shows the designs that the masters must carve in amber. Six tons of amber are needed, but unlike Jurassic Park fans the restorers do not want dinosaur hairs or million-year-old insects preserved within the resin. One ton confiscated from smugglers was donated by ex-Prime Minister Chernomyrdin, but most of this haul was not of the quality needed for the high standard of work. It has taken one year to finish just one panel, which has been on exhibition in Washington DC and Japan to raise awareness of the Amber Room and funds to rebuild it.

ABOVE: *Each piece of amber is fitted into place like a jigsaw puzzle, without the use of glue. One kilo of raw amber costs around $500, but a single large piece of high quality can cost up to $400. 92% of the world's amber is found in Kaliningrad.*

OPPOSITE PAGE: *One of the rebuilt panels. The freshly cut amber is quite a bright yellow, so it is coloured with a natural dye to achieve the rich, golden brown of old amber. As the amber darkens with time, so the dye fades and the natural colour takes over.*

AVTOVO METRO

Work began on the Leningrad metro in 1940, but because of the war and its aftermath trains only began running on November 15, 1955. The first kilometre of line was between Vostanie Square and Avtovo, and the decor of these stations was ornate and grand. Later interiors were more simple – unlike the Moscow metro, which began in the 1930s with 'Palaces for the People', and continued with grand architectural designs right up to the 1960s.

An early proposal to build an underground road in St Petersburg came from an imaginative resident, Torgovanov. His project for a tunnel, from the centre of the city to Vassilievsky Island, was rejected by Alexander I, who ordered the innovator to sign a pledge 'not to engage in hare-brained schemes in the future, but to exercise his efforts in matters appropriate to his estate'. Other similar projects were put forward around this time, but each section of society had a reason not to encourage them. The nobility stated that the excavation works would 'violate the amenities and respectability of the city', the landlords thought underground traffic would weaken building foundations, and the merchants feared that 'the open excavations would interfere with normal trade'. The most violent adversaries were the clergy, who insisted that 'the underground passages running near church buildings would detract from their dignity'.

The Leningrad metro was difficult to build; the land is swampy, the Neva deep and builders had to break through Cambrian clay dating back 600 million years. The stations served a double purpose – each had a gate to seal the underground so it would become a shelter if an atomic bomb fell. Every station has its own theme, reflecting either its name or the destination of the line. Kirovsky Zavod, the station for the Kirov Factory, is devoted to industrialization; Pushkinskaya, servicing the town of Pushkin, has a sculpture of the poet against a lyrical landscape of Tsarskoe Selo park.

The Classical domed pavilion of Avtovo station is not far from where the front line passed during the Siege of Leningrad. Around the base of the dome is an inscription in

ABOVE: *The end of the platform hall is decorated with a mosaic of a young mother holding her child, a symbol of peace.*

OPPOSITE PAGE: *Avtovo station, one of the first opened in 1955. Avtovo was the name of the Finnish village located here in the time of Peter the Great. Sixteen of the columns supporting the roof of the platform are clad in moulded glass panels, used here for the first time and proving just as hard-wearing as marble. The inner surface of the glass was cut at an angle and pressed onto the concrete shafts, so the facets reflect the light and the columns appear to be made of solid glass.*

gold: 'Eternal Glory to the brave defenders of Leningrad who withstood the enemy attacks on the hero city!', and chandeliers and lamps are decorated with laurel branches, gilded swords and other images of military valour. This station is not deep,

so it has a flat roof over the platform supported by 46 columns, and passengers descend via a grand, semi-circular staircase.

The metro is used by millions of people every day; the four lines are the central arteries of the city. At rush hour wagons are packed, while late at night one can sit alone. On Sundays they are filled with people returning from dachas laden with baskets of fruit or berries. The trains travel fast and regularly; they are probably the most efficient element of St Petersburg today.

PLANETARIUM & PULKOVO OBSERVATORY

The Planetarium is a very odd place – the third floor is now a wax museum, and at weekends the main hall is a discotheque. The administrators don't quite know who allowed the disco in, but it attracts young people. The Director told me it was like the West allowing night-clubs in churches: the 'cosmos', I suppose, was the Soviet equivalent to a sacred place.

The Planetarium was built in 1959, re-using the iron carcass of the St Petersburg Pavilion from the 1899 Nizhny-Novgorod Industrial Exhibition. Astronomy is on the school curriculum, and the subject of space is one of national pride. The first sputnik was developed in 1957, and probably the greatest hero of post-war Russia is Yuri Gagarin, who beat the Americans into space.

Another place connected with space in St Petersburg is the Pulkovo Observatory. Since 1805, the cannon that marks noon has been fired on a telegraph signal from the Observatory. From the Pulkovo Hills, stars have been studied on cold Russian winter nights since the 19th century. Pulkovo and Pulkovo Hills were often mentioned in wartime reports, because of severe fighting here during the Siege of Leningrad.

RIGHT: *The Museum of Astronomical Observation Instruments, known as* Man Conquers Space, *in the Planetarium in pre-Revolutionary Alexandrovsky Park. One small room contains a few dusty exhibits dedicated to the history of astronomy. Inside are two rare exhibits, an original 9m Foucault pendulum, that shows the rotation of the Earth, and a maquette made in 1914 of the first space rocket, made by Tsiolkovsky.*

OPPOSITE PAGE: *The Planetarium observation hall seats 480 people, under a semi-spherical dome 25m in diameter, made of aluminium plates covered with several layers of fibreglass. The Star Hall is the largest in Europe – the astronomical museum is minuscule in comparison.*

BELOW: *In the centre of the Star Hall of the Planetarium stands an optical apparatus manufactured by the Carl Zeiss Enterprise in Jena, in eastern Germany. It contains more than 100 projectors which recreate a picture of the stellar heavens.*

OVERLEAF PAGE 190: *A 26" refractor at Pulkovo Observatory, made by Carl Zeiss of Jena in the 1930s. Hitler wanted to present this to Mussolini. The original telescope was destroyed, but the lens was saved and after the war the International Astronomical Committee decided to present it to Pulkovo. It was restored by German specialists and given to Leningrad in the 1950s.*

Pulkovo's central Classical building is surrounded by large mushroom-like domes housing the telescopes and refractors. When the Soviet Union made the world's biggest telescope, there was great excitement in the scientific world. Its 6m-diameter reflector was 1m larger (Russians always have to be bigger to be better) than the diameter of the biggest telescope at the Mount Palomar Observatory in California.

Scientists used the powerful new telescope for the exploration of the universe. Without employing any additional devices, it enabled astronomers to take photographs of the 22nd and 23rd magnitude. These could previously be recorded only by radio-telescopes, and they apparently had not yet been catalogued at Mount Palomar. In Soviet days these two observatories were great rivals, but now the Pulkovo is badly in need of funding and welcomes foreign input. Soviet government spending on the space programme was huge, to keep their prominent position in the space race. Now it is minimal, focusing mainly on international projects, such as the space station Mir.

The world famous observatory, located on the meridian of St Petersburg, was also right on the front line and was reduced to ruins by the Nazis.

Soon after the war, the Leningrad Optical and Mechanical Factory – the only place in Russia producing astronomical instruments – was set up. Called the 'Astroshop' by workers, it brought the mangled instruments from the Observatory back to life. The Astroshop was the basis for LOMO – one of Leningrad's most successful factories, famous for producing cameras, microscopes and other optical equipment.

INSTITUTIONS

THE POSITIVE RESULTS OF COMMUNISM IN THE USSR were mainly due to the tremendous discipline and national identity enforced upon the people. After Khrushchev had repudiated the counter-productive influence of Stalin's god-like status in his 20th Party Congress Speech of 1956, the Soviet people could stop lurking in the shadows and start living openly. World-class musicians, ballet dancers, scientists and sportsmen were suddenly able to compete against their foreign counterparts. To work for the State was the fundamental root of the Soviet philosophy and this was instilled in the Russian citizen from childhood. The 'institution' provided a complete lifestyle, offering families health services, education and a social life. Perks were offered to good workers, such as holidays by the Black Sea or better housing. The education system was very strong; whether in specialized fields or elementary school, the standard was as high as top-ranking schools in other countries. As early as seven years old, gifted children were transferred out of the main education system and into special schools that concentrated on either sports, languages or the arts and sciences.

Under Khrushchev, there was a time of growing prosperity and a strengthening of the Soviet Union's international position. However, favoured members of the Politburo began to take advantage of their privileged positions, building luxurious private dachas and travelling abroad. By the time of Brezhnev in the 1960s, some leading Party members were corrupt and visibly lived in excess. Ordinary people sensed the unfairness but felt helpless to object, while talented citizens who had the chance defected. But the State still kept up its onslaught of propaganda and its people, along with the rest of the world, continued to believe in the global power of the Soviet Union.

VAGANOVA BALLET ACADEMY

Probably the most famous export from the city of St Petersburg is its ballet and the ballet school on Theatre Street produces talented dancers for the world. Some of its stars date back to the time of the Imperial Theatre School: Anna Pavlova, Vaslav Nijinsky, Mikhail Fokine, Georges Balanchine, Mathilda Kshesinskaya and Agrippa Vaganova herself. Even throughout the Soviet era (when the school was known as the Leningrad State Choreographic School), great names of ballet came from this formal training: Galina Ulyanova, the pride of Soviet ballet, and the defectors

who became internationally acclaimed: Natalia Makarova, Rudolf Nureyev, Mikhail Baryshnikov.

The Russian School of Theatrical Dance was founded in 1738 by decree of Empress Anna. The first ballet master, Jean-Baptiste Lande, taught the 'foreign steps' to 12 boys and 12 girls on an upper floor of the Winter Palace. Tsar Nicholas I loved the ballet, often giving up his seat in the royal box to sit in the first row. During his reign, in 1836, the Imperial Ballet School was given its current premises in Theatre Street, built in 1832-5 during the time of architect Carlo Rossi's magnificent town planning. Despite name changes and evacuation during the war to Perm, the school is one of the few buildings whose purpose has never altered.

The girls wore a uniform of a long, cornflower-blue dress with white collar and apron, but if a student achieved particular distinction in class, they were given a rose-coloured frock. Once in the academic year the Tsar would visit for a performance; it was during such a visit that Alexander III picked out Mathilda Kshesinskaya.

Ballet, until the early 20th century and the emergence of new choreographic techniques, was a very formal affair. Naked flesh was not permitted – in the *Dance of the Seven Veils* the dancers had to wear special tights with toes. Some of the original ballets are still studied and performed today, *Giselle* and *Coppelia* being probably the earliest from the French school. During the second half of the 19th century, Marius Petipa worked with Tchaikovsky on his three ballets that form the basis of the classical repertoire. Fokine was a graduate and professor of the school, although his success came later with the Ballets Russes and his collaboration with Sergei Diaghilev. Agrippa Vaganova, who taught at the school from 1921 to 1951, developed a teaching system emphasising harmony and co-ordination of the body, particularly the back, enabling her students to make soaring leaps and manoeuvre in the air. It was in recognition of her progressive teaching methods that in 1956 the school was renamed the Vaganova Ballet Academy and the students became known as 'Vaganovsky'.

Although foreign paying students can now attend, competition to enter the school is fierce, with over 4000 applicants for 70 places and high standards of physical and facial appearance. The discipline remains strict, creating dancers poised and prepared for their future debut on the ballet stages of the world.

LEFT: *The beautiful little girls, who curtsey politely to both visitors and teachers, sometimes seem too small and delicate for the roughness of everyday life.*

OPPOSITE PAGE: *The Mariinsky Theatre, home of the Kirov Ballet, where top students perform the child roles. The floors of the ballet studios at the Vaganova School were built to slope at the same angle as the stage of the Mariinsky.*

BELOW & BOTTOM: *The young dancers are trained like neophytes in religion, the discipline more rigid than in any military academy.*

CIRCUS

Whilst investigating the buildings of St Petersburg, a new picture of the city has formed. Now I know what stood where, and as I pass I look at places with new eyes. One such example is the Mariinsky Theatre, now the home of the Russian ballet, but which from 1849 to 1859 was the Imperial Circus Theatre. And on the Fontanka where the Chinizelli Circus now stands was the French Turnière Circus, a wooden building used mainly for puppet and magic shows. By 1847, the wood was so rotten it was sold as scrap. As a result of this, in 1877 on the initiative of Gaetano Chinizelli, a member of an Italian circus family living in Russia, the first stone circus in Europe was built.

Designed by Vassily A. Kenel (favourite architect of Grand Duke Vladimir), the theatre followed the basic principle of circus building: the ring has to be 13m in diameter, so the horses reach the correct angle and speed for the acrobats to perform on their backs. Kenel echoed this dimension in the cupola over the roof, the interior of which was painted with illustrations of circus acts. The building had large stables, since in those days horses were the main attraction. There were also living quarters for the large Chinizelli family – the three sons and three daughters each played a role in the circus troupe. The family continued to manage the circus until 1919, when Chippioni, the youngest son and last director, emigrated with his family to Italy and the Soviet Government took control.

Until Soviet times, the circus was filled mainly with touring troupes from Italy, Germany, Holland, France and England. The tradition of the circus was begun in England, by a Guards Officer, Philip Astley, who showed acrobats on horseback. The Government opened an Institute for Circus Workers, where any Soviet citizen could learn clowning, acrobatics and animal training without belonging to the traditional circus families. All circus workers were based in Moscow and sent to circuses across Russia for a set time. The famous Moscow State Circus was not made up of Muscovites, but of the crème de la crème of performers from all over the Soviet Union, hence its very high standard. Already new generations of

LEFT: *Animals such as elephants, zebras and hippopotami are bought from abroad, but camels, tigers and bears can all be found in regions of Russia. The trainers invent fairy tales to amuse the children, who, without prejudice, adore the glitter of the circus and the opportunity to see beautiful animals close up.*

OPPOSITE PAGE: *The 120th anniversary of the opening of the Chinizelli Circus was in 1997. The decor of the ring is changed regularly, for different shows.*

circus families have begun in Russia. The famous Kolya Pavlenko, with his beautiful troupe of tigers, began as assistant to Alexandrov-Fedotov in the 1950s. Alexandrov-Fedotov started the troupe, and some of his original cats still survive. This troupe, and that of Yuri Kuklachov with his performing domestic cats, are unique acts in the Circus world.

The famous Chinizelli Circus is a lime green building with white stucco and a neon sign. Russia is still a long way from the European trend of circuses without animals, but the animals are better off than those in zoos – their trainers treat them as part of the family and the circus still receives Government funding for food. When the band strikes up and the lights dim, the circus transports me back to childhood. I scream at the thrills of the trapeze and the tightrope, and chortle like a child at the ridiculous clowns. The Chinizelli Circus still has all the magic of a traditional Big Top, yet one never has to wait for it to come to town – it is permanently there in St Petersburg.

LESGAFT SPORTS INSTITUTE

LEFT: *A typical Socialist Realist mural decorates the main staircase, showing the heroism of sportsmen and women in an allegorical way. The composition of the picture is comparable to paintings showing the Gods descending from Mount Parnassus.*

OPPOSITE PAGE TOP: *The library of the Sports Institute now replaces the large collection of naval books that Grand Duke Alexander kept on these mahogany shelves. The portrait to the left of the doorway is of the famous pre-Revolutionary biologist, Peter Franzevich Lesgaft, after whom this Sports Institute is named. He dreamed of setting up an academy for specialists in Physical Education and opened the first training school for physical education teachers in 1893. Subjects such as anatomy, psychology and experimental physiology are on the curriculum, and graduates are qualified to teach sports in schools and universities, or work as professional trainers and coaches.*

In 1894, Tsar Alexander III presented the white Vorontsov palace on the Moika to his youngest daughter, Xenia, as a wedding gift. Here she lived with her husband, Grand Duke Alexander Mikhailovich (known in the family as Sandro), until in 1906 he fell in love with a 'woman' in Biarritz. Xenia was left heart-broken, but she continued to live in the palace with their seven children. It had been redecorated to her taste by Nikolai de Rochefort and Nikolai Sultanov around the original interior by Ippolito Monighetti. Monighetti's 'trademark' white marble staircase still remains in the entrance hall, but nowadays the steps squeak with the rubber soles of students, for the building is an Institute of physical culture.

Before the Revolution, most competitive sports began in St Petersburg in the military academies. The birth of Russian football was on September 13, 1897, when two St Petersburg teams played a match on the pitch belonging to the 1st Cadets Corps on Vassilievsky Island. Hockey, cycling, skating, gymnastics, weight lifting, sailing, skiing, tennis – all soon had their own clubs and teams. To the Proletkul'tists of the early 1920s, these sports derived from bourgeois society and were remnants of the decadent past and part of a degenerate culture. They condemned all sport 'tainted' by class society and went on to invent new games for children. The manufacture of dolls was stopped, because they were thought to foster a maternal disposition among young girls.

Sport in the Soviet Union was a political subject. The Communist Party believed it played an important role in social change, as regular exercise improved standards of hygiene, nutrition and public health. In 1928 the First Workers' Spartakiad for universal workers was staged, in answer to the 'bourgeois' Olympics held in Amsterdam that same year. The Supreme Council of Physical Culture imposed exercise breaks on industrial shop floors, and in the decade after the Revolution factory yards were often full of muscular men and women rhythmically swinging imaginary hammers and sickles, simulating work movements in time to music. In the 1930s, public squares were filled on national holidays with mass displays of gymnasts and athletes.

After the Second World War, sport became a recognized subject like a science and the teaching of professional sportsmen for international competitions began. It was only in 1952, in Helsinki, that the USSR competed in their first Olympic Games.

LEFT: *The small cabinet attached to a large oak library.*

LEFT: *The entrance hall was designed by Monighetti, and the elegant Classical decor seems out of place now it is full of muscle-bound youths with sports bags.*

SCHOOL

Schools for the Church had existed since the 16th century, but Peter the Great was the first to bring an element of state control into education. Of course the new schools were for the nobility, but they did later expand to include the children of soldiers, state officials and churchmen. Russians were encouraged to go abroad – particularly to England – to study at the state's expense. The true father of Russian education was Mikhail Lomonosov, son of a serf from the Archangelskoe area, who walked to St Petersburg in 1731 at the age of 20. He became a Russian Leonardo da Vinci, making significant contributions in the fields of chemistry, poetry, visual art, physics and mathematics.

Women had to wait until 1764 when Catherine the Great opened the Smolny Institute; her educational reforms were continued by Maria Feodorovna, wife of Paul I. From then on each Tsar opened new establishments for the ruling classes, but

it was only when Alexander II set up the Zemstvo (local governments) that the first schools opened in the provinces. Despite this, at the beginning of the 20th century the majority of the Russian populace was still illiterate. The most positive achievement of the Soviet State was to bring compulsory education to everyone, with more than 60% of the population completing high school and 30% going on to higher education.

Not all the new schools were purpose-built, many were set up in old buildings that had been appropriated by the State. For instance, in 1931, the former Swedish Reformation Church of St Catherine became one of the respected schools for physical education (Fizz Kult for short).

The Soviet standard of education was particularly high, emphasizing the sciences and Russian literature – although history was taught from a very biased perspective and geography was limited to the USSR. The schools also served the purposes of the ruling Communists; children were under constant political and ideological pressure, brought up from an early age to recite Lenin's doctrines such as: 'The school apart from life, apart from politics, is a lie and a hypocrisy.' At school, children were reminded continually of Lenin's catch-phrase from the Third Congress of the Young Communists' League in 1921: 'To study, study and study.' When asked, 'What are you supposed to study?', children had to answer, 'To study Communism.' which was followed by another Soviet cliché: 'You can only become a real Communist after studying all of mankind's wisdom.'

Even after the political reforms of the last decade the educational system remains very effective and mainly centralized, although there are economic problems with the payment of staff and provision of school meals. The wane of the Communist Party as the leading political force led to the removal of Marxist/Leninist ideology from the school curriculum, and somewhere along the line it was replaced by tuition promoting international ideas and introducing elements of the free market economy. Since the early 1990s

OPPOSITE PAGE: *In 1972 the former Swedish Church was divided into two levels, the lower becoming a basketball court and the upper a gymnasium. Here svelte girls champion their art; with balls, with ribbons, with hoops, they rehearse their Olympic routines. The girls – for only girls may train here – can attend classes between the ages of six and 16. Obviously the younger they start the better they become – although such exercises alter their figures and the older girls have the physique of a ten-year-old.*

alternative and private schools have begun appearing in Russia. These have visiting graduate teachers and offer students courses in Classical Latin and Greek and the chance to study abroad. The state schools are still strong in science and mathematics however – and are famous for generating a street-wise approach to all of life's possible problems.

ABOVE: *All the lost dreams of adults are placed in the young, each parent hoping that their child will have a chance at all that they missed.*

BELOW: *September 1 is the beginning of the school year – a national event, when parents bring their smartly-dressed children to school carrying bunches of flowers to present to the teachers. Welcoming speeches and introductions to new students and staff are usually held outside the school building, then a mad rush of excited children swarms into the school to study the programme for the year to come. The Galitzine Library arranged for an exchange visit between students of this school and those from Winchester College.*

MALUTKA

On a fine residential street off Liteiny Prospekt is a line of mansions that channel the journey through life. We begin with the palace for the registration of births, Malutka ('little baby'); two doors along is a ZAGS building for the registration of marriages, divorces and death; further down is a lawyer's office and next door a stonemason advertising marble gravestones.

Before the Revolution, the former Councillor of State owned the palatial home now known as Malutka. Built in 1895 by architect Alexander Pomerantzev, with an interior designed by Svinin, the building currently stands almost empty. Only a couple of offices hold registrars, waiting to receive the documentation of a new birth. Up the marble stairs, in a grand suite of rooms, ceremonies can be held – a civil celebration at which relatives gather and coo over the new addition to the family. A short speech is made, covering the duties of a new parent and offering wishes for the health and happiness of the child, whilst the ever-present commercial photographer hovers like a vulture, ready to record the scene. The registration is free of charge, but the optional ceremony (plus trimmings) is not.

One room holds files for birth certificates of the area since 1965. In the 1970s over 14,000 births a year were registered; now the figure has halved to about 5-600 a month. In Soviet times, childless couples paid extra tax and motherhood was encouraged as a service to the State, with monthly allowances to those with three or more children. The sum was so minimal that mothers continued to work. They relied on the help of the babushka or on Yasli-sad - crèches where infants lie in rows, wrapped like papooses to sleep and cry. This did not mean that children were unloved, quite the reverse; they are treasured and family life often rotates around them. Nowadays the economic situation has worsened and despite legal entitlement to maternity leave, fewer women are choosing to have children. Babies have been left on the steps of the Palace Malutka entrance, just as they are often left abandoned in trains. There is government help for single mothers: they receive

LEFT: *The Moorish boudoir is now used as a backdrop for group photographs – its alcove offers an excellent frame for mother and baby. The neighbouring room has been converted into a baby changing area and the Winter Garden, designed by the famous architect Kitner, is used for champagne receptions after the ceremony.*

LEFT: *The cherubs on the ceiling are part of the original decor by Svinin, but seem appropriate for the building's new use. Married mums receive child allowances for the fourth and subsequent children until they are five; allowances for unmarried mums begin with the first child. Children are divided into legitimate and fatherless (the term illegitimate is not used); the latter have no claims on the father.*

LEFT: *One of the rooms in the grand suite on the first floor, where celebrations of the birth can be held. The relatives gather and coo over the baby, probably oblivious to the elaborate interior around them.*

free kindergarten, a guaranteed job and help with housing payments, but if the man registers his fatherhood these privileges are retracted and technically he must pay child-maintenance. However, there is no follow-up service to ensure payment. This chauvinist law remains unchanged from Soviet times, when from 1918 to 1944 all children were legitimate and the responsibility for a child's upbringing was officially shared between the family and society at large. The child was expected to side with society against his family – as in the famous case of Pavlik Morozov, given hero status after he had denounced his father for forging documents and selling favours.

PALACE OF WEDDINGS

T he recently restored Palace of Weddings on Petrogradsky side was built in 1910 and, until 1917, was the private property of Grand Duke Nicholas Nikolaevich Jnr. He was first cousin once removed to Tsar Nicholas II and my father's godfather. My grandfather had been orphaned as a young child, and he and his brother were sent to live near Tula on their maternal uncle's estate,

Yakshino, which happened to be next door to the Grand Duke Nicholas' hunting grounds of Pershino.

The Grand Duke's Montenegrin wife and her sister were responsible for introducing Rasputin to the Court. When Rasputin gained the Empress' trust he warned her that the fate of Russia was doomed with Nicholas as Commander-in-Chief of the Army. Through her influence on the Tsar, Nicholas

OPPOSITE PAGE: *From a balcony above the Room of Ceremonies, the spooky sound of a Hammond Organ drones 'Here Comes the Bride' as the couple enter.*

ABOVE & RIGHT: *In the height of the marriage season, May to September, there are four registrations every hour and on a Saturday two or three couples can often be found waiting as though in a queue.*

was removed from office and sent to the Caucasus as viceroy and commander of the Russian forces fighting the Turks, the allies of the Germans in the First World War. The Grand Duke and other members of the royal family were later imprisoned in the Crimean fortress of Dulber, and from here they were rescued by a detachment of German troops – Lenin had made peace with the enemy. The Dowager Empress

Maria Feodorovna, also at Dulber, refused to receive the German commander. In April 1919, King George V sent two British warships, HMS *Grafton* and *Marlborough*, to rescue his cousin the Dowager Empress and her fellow prisoners. The ship arrived expecting to pick up seven or eight adults and some children and found 73 waiting on the quay, with over 300 tons of luggage!

Now the old palace of Grand Duke Nicholas is full of brides. There is nothing more romantic than a Russian Orthodox wedding, the service lit by candlelight and crowns held over the couple's heads. The Communist state replaced this beautiful, serious ceremony with the civil registration of marriage. For a man and woman to become a unit, all that is needed is a couple of witnesses and 15 minutes. Once registered, they can apply for independent housing (rather than having to share

with parents) and enjoy various financial perks at work, so 'marrying' is a necessary part of life.

Marriage in Soviet Russia had none of the connotations of Western Europe; most people married at least twice, the first time almost always in the mistaken rush of first love. Even the Russian Orthodox church had been quite liberal about this, allowing three church weddings for the man – although only one for the woman. Soviet society was a strange mix of prudishness and liberality, where prostitution was a way for women to gain financial independence, yet sex before marriage was considered improper until very recently. First-time brides are usually very young and excited but, by the third time, the women turn up as though to a dentist's appointment with children from former liaisons as guests. This, of course, happens the world over, but not quite so frequently as in Russia. The ladies who organize the wedding 'service' treat the baby brides more protectively than the older ones.

It is, most definitely, the woman's day – the husbands in their dark suits look sombre next to flower-bedecked girls. For a participant or friend there is excitement and hope of happiness for the newly-weds, but to a detached onlooker the young people seem like victims of the conveyor belt of society. The Master of Ceremonies (by Soviet tradition, always a woman), wearing red and looking like a Moonie priest, is usually more dolled-up than the mother-in-law. In Communist days, the couple had to promise to serve the State together; now they have to sign an agreement with the video cameraman for the film of the moment. The strange uncouthness of commercialism has crept into this once very solemn place. In a special room the couple and guests can watch the ceremony ten minutes after it actually happened – just in case they missed the reality. The wedding party then move on to the reception, to drink vodka and shriek at the newly-weds to KISS! As I sat waiting for the fluffy brides to pile up in the ante-chamber and watched each new surge of guests, I realized that the whole state of marriage in Russia today is about sex and housing.

DACHA

For dacha, read summer cottage, weekend retreat – any building not used as a full time residence. It can be anything from an extravagant, miniature palace decorated with marble and the finest silks, to what is little more than a wooden shed, without running water, electricity or telephone. The majority are built from wood and boast rather less in the way of ornate gilding, but a dacha is much more a state of mind, a restfulness, a certain atmosphere, a symbol of the peculiarly Russian genius for country living.

The tradition of the Russian dacha began with the Tsars, when the Imperial Court would transfer from the town to the countryside for the summer months. Even in those days the furnishing of the dacha tended to be rather spartan, and Catherine the Great travelled with a convoy of furniture. Rural life in Russia is an essential part of the culture and more often than not the dacha is built from scratch, using Soviet manuals to install a brick stove and build a roof. Every weekend, the train stations of St Petersburg are crowded with families

laden with construction materials and tools. A dacha can take years to build, summer being the only window of DIY opportunity, but for the past 70 years they offered the sole means of home-ownership for the average Russian. The dacha is almost exclusively a summer residence, because long, snow-covered winters are not exactly conducive to living in a draughty, wooden, stove-heated hut.

Keeping a good dacha requires a lot of hard work. The small plots of land average 600sqm, but invariably produce an annual crop of potatoes, carrots and cabbages. In addition, the surrounding countryside is full of wild berries to pick and mushrooms to gather. All this natural bounty is not only enjoyed fresh, but pickled, marinated and dried to be stored throughout the winter – such home-made foods always taste more delicious. According to a survey mentioned in the *St Petersburg Times*, the average Russian grows 38% of his food himself.

The dacha is not just a source of food, but an important part of life for the whole family. Grannies enjoy the cosy comfort of a village atmosphere, babies and toddlers benefit from clean air and sunshine, teenagers socialize around a campfire. At weekends, mum and dad arrive from the city to breathe fresh air and dig the garden. 'Dachniki' sunbathe, drink, go skinny-dipping, fishing and hiking, enjoy saunas and shashlik. The dacha is to the Russian what aspirin is to the Westerner – a

ABOVE & TOP RIGHT: *This modern dacha is designed in a very traditional style. The warmth of natural wood and the simple, bright furnishings give a very homely feel.*

cure for a host of minor ailments.

These days country sounds will inevitably be broken by the squawk of a New Russian's car alarm, or the ring of a mobile phone, but still the nightingale sings and the dreaded mosquitoes hum. This gently lyrical pastoral existence lasts a mere three months a year, but it builds people's strength for the long winter and the hard slog of tough urban life.

MARKETS

Colourful and enlivened by the different nationalities of the CIS, the market is always a good gauge of the prosperity of Russia. Here one finds the bustle of Eastern Russia and the house-proud orderliness of the Baltic States. Dark faces, gold teeth chewing dried apricots, Armenians, Georgians, Chechens - all with their own dialects or languages. Babushkas, who can't afford the stall price, stand outside selling a bunch of radishes from their own garden or

fresh milk from their pet goat or cow and a rural feeling is brought to this architecturally sophisticated city.

The oldest markets are Nikolsky market on Ulitsa Sadovaya and Andreevsky market on Vassilievsky Island, both built in the late 18th century. As the city grew, more markets sprang up and in Soviet times these centres of trade were reconstructed for the produce of the collective farms. Lenin's New Economic Policy allowed the right of free trade in agricultural produce,

limited at first to local fairs and marts. By 1923 the NEP-men had come into existence, as a medium through which trade between town and country was re-established. Only a few years after the Revolution a division between wealthier and poor peasants had developed, so a progressive scale of taxation was invented to mollify the Party's conscience. The more land a peasant planted, the greater the surplus of grain above his sales quota, and this extra was subject to higher tax – not a good incentive to make the land more prosperous. In Stalin's first years in office, government goals became higher and more peasants were forced into the collective farm system, either by necessity or coercion.

Throughout Soviet times the markets were an island of free enterprise within the socialist state. People from all walks of life could be found selling or haggling over their wares and those involved developed an understanding of the power of cash. Many members of the so-called Russian 'Mafia' began their wheeler-dealing in this way. An entrepreneurial student would earn extra money in the summer months by bringing fruit to market. In the late summer or autumn, a city dweller could find a collective farm or village with fruit trees, not too far from the train station, and pay to pick their fruit, sleeping in a nearby barn or paying a small sum for a bed. After gathering over 200kg of fruit or vegetables (less was not worth the effort) they would return to the city and sell the produce at market. One needed a collective farm work permit, which could be obtained for a bottle of vodka and about 20 roubles (a lot of money then). The produce has always been checked by the hygiene inspector and is stored near the market. Usually most is sold within two to three days. The fruits and vegetables are grown without chemicals and therefore sometimes look less appetizing than Western supermarket food, but they taste better. In 1989, when there was little more than a cabbage in the shops, the markets sold apples from Bulgaria, oranges from the southern states and the occasional lemon or grapefruit. I was warned to avoid oversized carrots and beets from Belorussia, as the wind from Chernobyl had blown over these crops. Now the markets are full of sellers, not only from all over the CIS, but also bringing imported goods from Europe. Restaurateurs employ shoppers to comb the huge selection for the best deal, and a visit to the market reminds one of the opulent days of 1913.

ABOVE: *Fish, meat and dairy produce are also sold, along with flowers and traditional handicrafts.*

RIGHT & FAR RIGHT: *In the summer months, the markets have a bigger variety of fruits and vegetables, but all year round you can find fresh food when the shops have none.*

OPPOSITE PAGE:
Each region of the city has its own market, usually situated in a purpose-built warehouse.

BANK

At the beginning of the 20th century, the bulk of Russia's wealth was held in the Imperial Treasury. After the Revolution, capital was collected for redistribution among the people. For almost the entire 20th century, banking in Russia has been centralized. In 1913, Imperial Russia was the richest country in Europe. The natural resources of the Urals were sold internationally and the developing railroad system created enormous profits. Banks built luxurious buildings to impress multi-national clients, with rows of full safe deposit boxes in the basement. However, much of this prosperity came via Germany and Central Europe, and had little time to develop before the outbreak of the First World War.

The General Treasury was originally located in a Quarenghi building on the Griboedev Canal, which now houses a school of economics. In 1912, as a result of the developing economic boom, a competition was set up for a new building to house the Head Treasury and main St Petersburg Savings Bank. The winning design, by D. Iofan, S. Korvin-Krukovsky and S. Serafimov, was built on the Fontanka between 1913 and 1915. This building is one of the few banks that continued to store money in Soviet times, when it was the Leningrad branch of the Government Bank.

Archive documents show that Lenin and his Bolshevik Party were receiving funding from the Nazis during the First World War, although the Communist Party claimed they were forged. This was intended to foment internal unrest in Russia, resulting in Nazi victory; instead it accelerated the collapse of the monarchy and created a strong patriotic front to defeat the enemy. After the Bolshevik Revolution of 1917, the pent-up frustrations of workers were released in enthusiastic looting and pillaging. The last Director of the Imperial Treasury, Ivan Pavlovich Shipov, was held at gun point and made to hand over keys to all the private safe deposit boxes. In each bank were jewels and deposit bonds; together with all the treasures found in private houses, everything was taken on behalf of the people.

By the end of the Brezhnev era, people were again becoming dissatisfied with their lot. The ideology of communism and equal distribution of wealth had visibly not worked, Party leaders lived in private dachas with limousines and servants – how was this different to Grand Dukes in chauffeur-driven Bugattis?

With the emergence of a black market, the Soviet economy eventually collapsed and the Government was forced to take on a free market economy. For those who had been well-positioned in Communist times this meant an opportunity to get rich

RIGHT: *Designed by D. Iofan, S. Korvin-Krukovsky and S. Serafimov, the Central Government Bank has a domed glass roof over the stairs and another over the operations hall, which must now be a security nightmare. The original safe deposit boxes lining the basement are still used.*

quick, storing their money out of Russia in tax havens. For most people, making a profit was still considered as speculation and therefore caused a bewildering moral dilemma – in Soviet times speculation was a criminal offence. For seven years Yeltsin's government experimented with economic reforms, even going so far as adding and then dropping several noughts to the rouble denomination. Nothing much helped to support the worthless rouble, and billions of dollars left Russia. The new banking systems were an administrative nightmare – at one point there were 72,000 different banks, leading to bankruptcy for the majority of course. In 1998, when the roof of the falsely-created exchange rate was removed and the Central Bank refused to make payments on State Bonds, Russia's new economy collapsed.

Despite the erratic nature of their profession, Armani-clad bankers still weave their way through the changing rules and boundaries, whilst an army of babushkas in blue housecoats clean the marble staircase, confused by the high prices in the shops, but glad of a job in an evermore uncertain future.

RIGHT: *The 3000sqm operations hall is one of the largest halls in the city, and has decorative parts from every major architectural period of the 20th century.*

OPPOSITE PAGE: *As banking in Russia is such a relatively new profession, the rules are continually changing and bankers train as they work, attending lectures in this hall.*

LOMBARD

Lombard means pawnbroker in Russian. The use of the pawnbroker is a part of Russian culture that has existed unchanged since the end of the 18th century. The wife of Paul I, Maria Feodorovna, was put in charge of the one pawnshop that existed for the city – conversely situated in Millionaires' Street. By the 1820s there were six shops, all of which were branches of the central Lombard.

A passage in the *James' Journal* of 1816, mentions: 'The Russian nobility's expenditure not infrequently exceeds their means'. R. Lyall, adds, 'Generally exceeds them: for almost all the nobility are in debt and have their estates pledged to the Lombard'. For the non-landowning classes, using a pawnbroker was the normal way of balancing income; when the warmer months arrived, the fur coat would be pawned to cover the extra expenses accumulated through the winter. Journalists and authors often needed to pawn a watch, or a silver trinket, whilst searching for a publisher or reaching a deadline. Dostoevsky described the use of money lenders – not just for his own survival, but as the integral theme in *Crime and Punishment*; Raskolnikov murders the old woman to whom he is pawning his watch. Such independent money-lenders gave a better deal than the official pawn shops, who had to pay a percentage to the central office.

The Deux Français, who visited St Petersburg in 1791-92, described the Lombard on Millionaires Street: 'one first finds two rooms which look small for their purpose; in one are put the pawned effects, and sales are held there; in the other are the valuers and the cashiers who pay out the money. They get jewels brought to them, fabrics and skins of all sorts, no longer carriages as they have no room to put them in. They lend against diamonds a third or at least a quarter of their value, they are sometimes brought settings worth 30-40,000 roubles. One pays 6% interest for land and houses; these last are pledged for one to five years. The funds of this establishment are 16 million roubles and the turnover in a normal year is estimated at 45 million.'

The Lombards were privately run after 1914, but this system of money-lending was stopped after the Revolution and their safes and storerooms were raided. In 1921, the NEP reintroduced a strictly controlled private enterprise system in limited areas, to speed up the economy after the devastating effects of world and civil war. The demand for loans was so great, that in 1923 the centralized pawnbroker reopened to offer State-controlled credit and has existed ever since – 1998 was its 75 year anniversary. Because there was one centralized savings bank and often people had more valuables than cash, the pawn shop remained active – especially in times of crisis. In 1992/3, when the old rouble notes were removed from circulation, there was a sudden rush to the pawnbroker, as suddenly paper money was worth nothing but objects gained in value.

As many as 60% of clients are regulars, but each is too shy to look into the pawnbroker's eyes and they always say it is their first visit. It is a pathetically sad sight to see an old lady slip her gold wedding ring across the counter, in order to buy groceries for the next month.

ABOVE: *In these sometimes wonderful interiors, there is a strange spirit of despair, mixed with an aura of uneasy decisions and betrayed memories, the human tragedies and fecklessness that have brought the pawnbroker's clients here.*

LEFT: *The staircase is lit by an oval skylight. From 1805, this building was occupied by the Russian-American Company, who financed ventures in Alaska. K. Ryleev, a leading Decembrist lived in a company flat on the ground floort.*

OPPOSITE PAGE: *Today, most of the pawnbroker's clients are state employees, whose salaries are late. The main items pawned are wedding rings and gold teeth, on which the owner receives 80% of the valued price, and pays interest of ½% of the value of the loan per day. Every two months they must sign a new agreement or buy back their property, but 10-15% of borrowers never return.*

ABOVE: *Detail of the ceiling in the Director's office.*

DOM RADIO

Radio has long been the 20th century's main form of communication. Soviet cities had 'Big Brother' speakers on each street corner, reminding citizens of their allegiance to the State, making people proud to work for their country. Every apartment was automatically furnished with a 'kitchen radio' with its own special wall plug; the city radio would burst forth without any choice of station. Since 1992 independent commercial stations with foreign backing have sprung up and renovation of flats has removed the otherwise useless plugs, diminishing the once vast audience to a minimum. City radio programmes are more intelligent than those provided by the pop stations, but unfortunately they are not on FM wavelength.

Dom Radio houses the State radio stations, Radio St Petersburg and Radio Russia (when broadcast from St Petersburg). It has always been strictly security conscious — live shows are only a very recent development; in Communist times material was checked and edited before transmission. The origin of the radio building is uncertain; it was possibly commissioned by a Japanese firm in 1911. The architects, Vassily, Vladimir and George Kosyakov, won a national competition in 1912 set up by the St Petersburg Noble Merchants Assembly. The outbreak of the First World War meant that the house was immediately used as an infirmary by the Japanese Red Cross

LEFT: *The facilities and methods of editing are still very old fashioned: scissors and spools of tape. There was a pioneer element when creating my show and it was fun using the ancient equipment, working late into the night with the sound engineer.*

ABOVE: *What is now the main orchestral recording studio was once a huge ballroom, with columns and decorative balconies, which could have held over 600 people.*

LEFT: *A small museum in the building commemorates the history of radio in the Second World War. Leningrad Radio played its own major part, transmitting the constant beat of a metronome over the town speakers to reassure people that it continued to function. The beat would get faster when there was an air raid and it was unsafe to walk on the streets.*

OVERLEAF PAGE 216: *There are oriental influences in the decor, and an oil painting of the 'Goddess Diana Hunting' on the ceiling.*

(which may account for the Japanese association), until 1918.

In 1924 the famous words 'Govorite Leningrad' (Leningrad speaks) were heard on the airwaves, and the history of Russian radio began. During the Second World War, even in hunger, at least one programme a day was transmitted, whether musical, radio play, reading or a topical discussion. On August 9, 1942, Leningrad proved that, despite the blockade and the deprivations of war, art had not died: the first performance of Shostokovich's Seventh Symphony was transmitted live from the Philharmonia. The programme could be picked up on short-wave radio as far away as London and Latin America. The orchestra was composed of musicians serving in nearby trenches, who were given special provisions from Gastronom No. 1. The main transmitter was later moved from the centre of town to the Buddhist Temple, after a bomb hit the neighbouring building, smashing Dom Radio's windows.

When I arrived in Leningrad in 1989, there was still an element of isolation, a motherly protection against Western information. In 1990 I suggested a programme about English music to the main producer of the Leningrad Youth Channel. It seemed to me that Russian knowledge of pop music was like a record stuck on Pink Floyd and Led Zeppelin. I pre-recorded a series of four programmes in my then limited Russian, from my own cassette collection. The shows were a huge success and each time I arrived in Russia, I would record more. In London I had access to all main labels' stock – the programmes had a potential audience of 260,000,000 people.

Eventually pre-recording became too time-consuming and when I was offered a live show on a new local station, I accepted. My days at Dom Radio were over, I had defected to the new wave of commercialism. The novelty of having a radio show wore thin, however, when the cost of my excess baggage – full of CDs and records – was more than my wages! I realised it was time to let native Russian speakers take over.

NEW RUSSIA

The CIS has only existed since the 1991 August coup, so it has been finding its feet and adapting to western politics and economic principles. Its people have emerged from 300 years of Romanov autocracy and 75 years of Soviet pressure that few in the West can comprehend. The largest country in the world is the possessor of a vast resource of raw materials, its population once had one of the highest standards of education in the world, sent rockets to the moon and developed the nuclear bomb, yet at the end of the 20th century the country is bankrupt and the people can barely feed themselves.

There has been a period of massive change, a time when rules were still unwritten and underground groups broke barriers in the arts. The elite of St Petersburg introduced Western trends and fashion but in a typically Russian way – adapting them to suit their needs, as they had done in previous centuries. For a time in St Petersburg it seemed that all the values of European civilisation could be realized on a higher plane. Soviet ideals were subjected to a lively sense of irreverence and new artistic communities popped up overnight like mushrooms.

Today Russia is somewhat less romantic. Most of the public buildings that were once conscientiously restored have fallen into a forlorn state of disrepair. The fortunate few, who were able to benefit from the uncertain state of post-coup Russia, have been able to privatize their homes and redecorate with imported furniture. The chasm between rich and poor has opened once again, the balloon of hope has burst and Russia is struggling and restless. When the State was the enemy, the people cheated the State; after it became 'democratic' the people saw little change and continued with their deceptions, forcing the centralized economy to collapse. Those who were once brought up in the confines of a rigid nationalism now have children who are unable to recognize Lenin. The New Russia needs to find a national identity - and nowhere more so than in St Petersburg, which is fast becoming a 19th-century façade hiding broken dreams.

BRIDGES

St Petersburg is based on 44 islands and 14% of the land-mass is covered with water, so bridges are a necessity. Footbridges, suspension bridges, wooden bridges; those across the Moika were originally painted bright primary colours, whereas the Fontanka had stern chain bridges designed by Perronnet. Peter the Great refused to allow bridges over the Neva river, as he feared they would obstruct passage to his port. Instead, barges were provided to ferry people across its wide expanse. With no access, his intention for the centre of the new capital to be on Vassilievsky Island, an isolated island in a deep river, failed. In 1727, after Peter's death, Isaac's Bridge became the first wooden bridge across the

Neva. It stretched from the embankment in front of the wooden St Isaac's Church across to Vassilievsky. It was a pontoon bridge, a deck mounted on anchored barges, which swung open to allow boats to pass. A toll was paid to cross, the price of which was based on weight. This bridge remained until 1916, when it caught fire from sparks sprayed by a passing tugboat.

The first permanent bridge, the Nikolaevsky (now Lieutenant Schmidt), was built in 1843-50. Ships could pass through seven of the iron arches, each with a drawbridge of a different width. The sculptors Klodt and Pimenov were invited to decorate the bridge and Bryullov designed fine wrought iron railings. After the embankments were covered in granite, bridges became more ornate, with iron railings, lanterns and even lions, griffins and sphinxes. In 1803, a second pontoon bridge was built, Trinity Bridge, linking the mainland to Petrogradsky Island. This was reconstructed in 1897-1903 as a lifting bridge, by the French Batignolles company, and was the longest bridge until the modern Alexander Nevsky Bridge was completed in the 1960s. The Trinity was opened with a short religious ceremony attended by the French President, Félix Faure, and the Tsar and Tsarina. It is still decorated with the original electric lanterns, but in 1934 was renamed the Kirovsky Bridge.

The Alexander Bridge (now Liteiny) was an engineering feat when it was built in 1874-79 for it is 57m high when raised; at night it looks like a dark skyscraper looming over Bolshoi Dom (the ex-KGB building and the highest roof in the area). The other impressive construction is the Bolshoi Okhtinsky, opened in 1911 and named the Peter the Great Bridge; the four heavy towers surrounding the drawbridge were designed by the architect Apishkov, with Leonti Benois acting as architectural consultant.

The Palace Bridge, by architect R.F. Meltzer and engineer A.P. Pshenitzky in 1912-16, was the last drawbridge to be planned before the Revolution. It was not finished due to the unrest, but in 1924 a wooden crossing was placed on the original ironwork and asphalt was finally laid in 1925. A major plan for a fountain on the Strelka spit and sculptures on the bridge, dated 1911, can be seen in the Central Archives.

In October 1917, Nikolaevsky Bridge was raised to stop sailors and workers from charging into the city, but after the cruiser *Aurora* took up a threatening position beside it, the bridge was

ABOVE & OPPOSITE PAGE: *Inside Palace Bridge, wheels and cogs prise the two sections of the bridge apart. The night shift works from 11pm to 6am, the Lieutenant Schmidt opening at 1.50am and the others within five minute intervals. People stay up late to watch them open in succession, like a row of dominoes.*

OVERLEAF PAGES 220 TO 221: *In winter, when the river is frozen, ships do not sail, but in the long White Nights, one of the most famous sights is the raising of the huge bridges across the Neva to allow cargo ships through to the Baltic Canal. Palace Bridge closes again for a break of 15 minutes around 3am to allow cars to pass; sometimes the traffic is like Manhattan at midday. For those caught on the wrong side of the river, the bridges are a wonderful excuse for staying out all night.*

lowered and the storming of the Winter Palace began. Many Revolutionary scenes took place on Trinity Bridge, since it linked the Bolshevik Headquarters in the Kshesinskaya Mansion to the mainland. The old British Embassy was located on the SE corner, and the observant Meriel Buchanan spent days watching the soldiers coming and going across the bridge.

BOILER ROOM

Until a few years ago, it was illegal to be unemployed in Russia. The boiler rooms of the city employed pensioners and those without higher education, and also provided work for the artists, musicians and writers of the 'underground', those who did not belong to any recognized union and needed some kind of work to keep officials off their backs. This work also had the almost unique attraction of not being affiliated to any labour collective, so employees did not have to attend political meetings and remained relatively unaffected by State pressures. Work was part-time, usually in 24-hour shifts, and the heating systems did not operate during the summer months, so there was plenty of free time to socialize, paint or rehearse. During working hours there was also time to read, write and occasionally stoke the fire, both literally and metaphorically.

Most of the heating in the city is centralized, and even today it is still subsidized by the government. It is automatically switched off in May – making a prolonged winter even more unpleasant – and switched on again around the beginning of October. In the early 1990s, when Government cuts were first made, the amount of power for heating was reduced, causing many complaints from pensioners and mothers with babies. The hot water system in most modern apartments is also centralized, and it is turned off for servicing for a month in the summer.

This particular boiler room has been immortalized, because the late Victor Tsoy, lead singer of the pop group Kino, once worked here. Tsoy was a Russian-Korean, who became a legend to his generation. The words of his songs were pure and simple, and illustrated very well what it was like to be a young person in Russia during this period. By the time of his death, in a car crash in the summer of 1990, the band was selling out stadium tours all over Russia. Groupies dressed like him, and hung out morning to evening in the courtyard round his boiler room, and also his home, covering the walls in graffiti and smoking soft drugs, much to the disconcertion of residents.

Today, if people have the opportunity, they install their own water heaters and new radiators with thermostats. Then they can feel entirely independent – with a choice as to when to switch appliances on or off, irrespective of whether the Government has decided that winter has begun or ended. With such fittings, an apartment is classed as Euro-standard and this can add several thousand dollars to its market price.

RIGHT: *Attached to the boiler room are small cosy rooms, which the 'kochegar' (heating mechanic) makes his own, sometimes inviting friends round to drink beer or vodka. Although technically it is against the rules to drink on the job, nobody checks.*

OPPOSITE PAGE: *This boiler is a coal and wood burner, although there are gas boilers as well. The furnaces are usually situated in the basements of the large buildings that they serve. The singer Victor Tsoy worked here shovelling coal, stoking the boiler, while he rose to fame. He starred in a film called* Igla, *which showed his place of work.*

CLUBS

Over the last few years an underground music culture has emerged in Russia. Since Glasnost and the appearance of 'rock stars' such as the late Victor Tsoy of Kino and Boris Grebenshchikov from Aquarium, young kids have ambitions to become new heroes. Suddenly it became easier to drop out of school, pick up a guitar and write words of dissatisfaction. The first public venue to accommodate this new phenomenon was the Leningrad Rock Club. It was also the official organization that read the text of all songs before giving permission for new groups to perform. This review was not about censorship but control – the KGB were always keen to know the root of any discord. Every year the Rock Club would stage its own festival, and because it was unique to Leningrad it is thought that the 'rock' scene began there.

Since 1988, as Western interest homed in on the Russian 'underground' music scene, the controls have become more lax, as has the standard of musicians. Untrained youths chose to stretch their vocal chords and hang out together drinking beer, in the belief that they were therefore a band. Russian men love to hang around in gangs – this may well be a significant factor in the success of the army, the pre-Revolutionary elite societies, and present day bandits. With the birth of new groups, for the first time new slang and new styles of clothing emerged, creating a harsh generation gap. Children no longer believed in the same ideology as their parents and the Communist system had to revitalize itself or be lost. Until this point, the patriotism and self-promotion of the Communist Party had proved victorious over each new generation; now suddenly teenagers wanted to speak the universal language of pop culture, where Soviet politics has little place.

As yet, a light entertainment industry has not developed in Russia, but public demand has produced young entrepreneurs with initiative; young people prepared to challenge the norm and begin a club in an unexpected location, on very little money. Clubs and discotheques are the latest cultural phenomenon taking over State altars, sports stadiums, swimming pools –

ABOVE: *The Fish Fabrique – an alternative rock club, set up in a squat by young musicians. Live music and a licence to sell alcohol mean that the place was filled at weekends.*

LEFT: *The $1,000,000 Club catered for the macho Russian male, with topless go-go dancers and 1970s disco lighting.*

ABOVE: *The Tunnel discotheque, located in a former bomb shelter, played progressive dance music. Much of the original decor was left, including water tanks behind the corrugated iron bar and the toilet system.*

RIGHT: *Pyramid is frequented by an older, professional crowd. The decor is based on an Egyptian tomb.*

even the Planetarium. The two Haas brothers requested permission from the Petrogradsky Regional Committee to redecorate and renovate an old bomb shelter as a discotheque. Permission had to be granted by the institution that had built and never used this shelter, but luckily the relevant officials found the idea fascinating – as well as obviously more lucrative than having the place sit empty waiting for a bomb. Through its style, The Tunnel found its own voice – being underground and a shelter, it attracted the young and radical people playing progressive sounds, becoming a legend throughout the night-club world of St Petersburg and Moscow. It was the forerunner of independent venues and also began the trend of bringing foreign DJs in to play for an evening.

Dancing has always been a Russian custom, and a night of beating the air and stamping one's feet is as good a work-out as an hour in a boxing ring – as well as a great stress reliever. Now, as in other places in Europe, the dance scene is a thriving industry. And, as most of its needs are imported, this is probably the most cosmopolitan set to be found in Russia. Drugs and alcohol are, of course, a factor and clubbers have ended up lying on the floor as the OMON do a violent narcotics search.

The OMON are the special-branch armed police – they look like tough paramilitary thugs and behave likewise.

Despite the noise and the darker side of club life, there is a positive aspect. At last there is a channel for young people to spend money at weekends. Although this puts enormous pressure on their parents – who are mostly unable to support their children beyond feeding them – it also creates an incentive for the young to work and earn their own money. As designers in many fields evolve – for interiors, for clothes, for posters and in the retail industry – so new shops and magazines are emerging. For those who are frustrated guitarists or drummers, the position of DJ offers an alternative role to aspire to. With no musical training, anyone can spin a few tracks and look very prepossessing in headphones and an offensive T-shirt.

The period of Glasnost and Perestroika saw 'youth culture' pandering to Western journalists eager for a scoop on the disintegration of Communism.

Now foreign cultures (such as the rock and club scene) have become part of the norm, with new Russian millionaires investing in the opening of night-clubs or new record labels; for the first time youth culture is not State controlled.

CASINO

In a restored mansion on Liteiny Prospekt, that once belonged to the Dolgoruky family, there is now a casino for New Russians. These two words describe a particular type that has appeared on the international scene since 1991. They evoke a picture of dark Mercedes drawing up outside expensive restaurants; groups of burly, bejewelled men in leather coats escorting designer-clad women swathed in fur; dinner bills of thousands of dollars being paid from briefcases full of cash. This is the type of Russian that the casino attracts, and – although they claim to offer membership to all – the rigid 'face-check' on the door dissuades an ordinary Russian from entering.

The Conti Group run the four leading casinos in St Petersburg and they have leased the Liteiny mansion. Built in 1843 by Andrei N. Nizovtsev, it was sub-divided into communal flats during Soviet times. Now the interior has been completely refurbished to its former luxury, and in rooms where several families once lived several thousand dollars can be lost on the turn of a card. There is a rouble hall and a valuty (foreign currency) hall, as well as a special VIP room where stakes are higher and privacy is guaranteed. Even so, everywhere one is watched by roving state-of-the-art security cameras.

In the world of casinos it is well known that Russians are great gamblers; their reckless natures can lead to disaster, sometimes for themselves, sometimes for the casino. Dostoevsky, himself a sufferer, wrote a book on the theme. Pushkin based the title character for his famous story, *The Queen of Spades*, on a Princess Galitzine who loved gambling.

ABOVE: *The Emerald Room at the Olympia Casino. This room is only for gambling in roubles, with a minimum stake of 50 roubles and a limit of 50,000.*

OPPOSITE PAGE: *Olympia has a luxury restaurant and a bar, and is open to members only.*

Catherine the Great often bailed out her favourites after they had been ruined at the card tables, and throughout history many an estate changed hands in similar circumstances. Russia is large, Russia is rich and the Russian nature is expansive; despite a Soviet ban on gambling these characteristics did not disappear. The Russian casino, even in times of economic crisis, is always filled with punters. As yet, however, no-one has equalled the extremes of the pre-Revolutionary aristocracy in extravagance: one Grand Duke, in the South of France and homesick for Russia, paid for troikas to be driven down boulevards sprinkled with rock salt to imitate snow, while Prince Yusupov sent his shirts from Petersburg to Paris to be laundered and winter balls in the capital often had temporary fountains flowing with champagne.

RIGHT: *The ultra-modern Conference Hall, aside from serving its intended purpose, has been used as a regular setting for TV chat shows and live performances for visiting businessmen.*

NEW ACADEMY

Since 1993, an apartment in a large squat off Nevsky Prospekt has been a sanctuary for lovers of Classical art. Set up by the artist Timor Novikov, the New Academy is a gallery offering a Classical training to its artists without a political influence, along the lines of Plato's private academy. Believing that art should be beautiful and that the modern art world is overrun with ugliness, Novikov encourages his contemporaries to use Classical form and rules of perspective. The walls of the gallery are delicately lined in pale blue silk, the studios painted cream and scattered with Classical torsos and Corinthian columns. It is the juxtaposition of historical and contemporary – scenes of Ancient Greece painted in acrylic, photographs of models dressed in togas with Doc Marten boots – that brings Greek Classicism into the context of the 20th century. Whether a collage of computer images or plaster casts of modern faces, the New Academicians are inspired by the past but produce work that is right up to date.

The house in which the New Academy is situated is known simply by its address: Pushkinskaya 10. This building has been a nucleus of creativity since 1989; its huge double courtyard is surrounded by six floors of empty apartments that were occupied by most of the unofficial artists and musicians of Leningrad during the time of Perestroika. It has been the bane of the City Council – the house was better occupied than left empty, but squatting was against the law. Over the years, the electricity and water supplies were turned off and eviction notices distributed, but the City had no money to renovate the premises or to deal with the 400 or so artists who would be left without studios, so they turned a blind eye to its existence. In summer, music festivals and exhibitions were held in the courtyard. At the end of 1996, the conditions became too extreme – no water, no heat, no light – and the last of the artists was evicted.

A few of the occupants were, by now, considered part of the city establishment – including the New Academy. Highly respected in the St Petersburg art world, the gallery was allowed to remain open and the electricity and water reconnected. Several works by members of the group are in the Russian Museum, which also hosts group shows and gives studio space for drawing classes in the Michael Fortress. The gallery holds exhibitions every alternate Saturday, as well as regular lectures and presentations. The New Academy gets a lot of media attention, both in the Russian and Western press, due to the cosmopolitan nature of the artists and their talent for self-promotion. Their work is obviously not Russian-orientated, yet as a group they are the strongest movement in the city. Timor Novikov and the New Academicians are committed to fighting the Modernist influences of 'Brit Pop' artists and the Moscow Radicals in the International Art Scene. Like Dostoevsky, it is their belief that 'Beauty will save the world.'

ABOVE: *An exhibition of the work of Georgie Guryanov, who takes famous Socialist Realist images and paints them in Technicolor - giving his work the look of glossy advertising rather than political propaganda.*

OPPOSITE PAGE: *Oleg Maslov and Viktor Kuznetsov work in partnership, recreating Classical myths and scenes in painting, photography or performance. Their work always includes self-portraits in Classical poses, and they make their own costumes.*

RIGHT: *Plaster casts of the heads of the artists of New Academy, surrounding that of their mentor, Timor Novikov. These are the work of Julia Strauss.*

ANIKUSHIN'S STUDIO

With the death of Mikhail Anikushin in May 1997, an era ended for Leningrad. He was the People's Sculptor, and true to his title he loved people and he loved his Russia. He rose to fame in 1949 when he won the Soviet Union's first-ever open competition, for a monument to Alexander Pushkin. Many who see this statue in the centre of Arts Square assume it is a 19th-century work, so well does it blend with the architecture. Like that of any true master, his work is timeless. After the 1991 coup, most statues of Lenin were removed – but not that by Mikhail Konstantinovich. It was a fine example of Soviet craftsmanship and beyond politics, so Lenin still stands on Moscow Prospekt, cap held out in a humanitarian gesture. Anikushin's other great work in the city is the *Monument to the Heroes of the Defence of Leningrad*, built 1968-75. This massive complex of statues stands in Victory Square, a powerful reminder to any visitor arriving from the airport of the city's bravery during the Siege. As a survivor, who saw so many die during the blockade, Anikushin felt that this was his war effort. His monuments also stand in prominent positions in many other Russian cities, and in Japan, India, Finland, China and Great Britain.

Anikushin's studio, an ugly concrete structure hidden in a small park, was built in a relatively quiet area of Leningrad in 1968. The building contains three studios, as his wife, Maria Timofeevna, is a sculptor in her own right, but the main area is the large studio, filled with the ghosts of ballerinas, astronauts, surgeons, generals, Lenins, Pushkins and Chekhovs. I posed for him during the first year of our friendship, sitting up high on a rotating platform in the cold grey light of Russian winter. He would only work in natural light, believing that electricity was not Classical. He used his hands to create shapes and images in the air, not waving them about but clutching the atmosphere as though moulding clay. We would listen to Caruso, crackling on an old 78-rpm gramophone, and it would gradually lull me into a dream state despite the cold. When working he paced to and fro, looking at both clay and subject from all angles. Every movement was definite, all

proportions were correct; from the first lumps of clay the head was recognizable. I was privileged to be taken under his wing and from 1989 worked alongside him. During my time spent in this inspiring place, I learnt by watching and occasionally the master would walk past saying, 'Don't rush, – look,' under his breath; they were the best lessons I ever had. He loved to work and was proud of what he called 'Peter's clay', the green clay upon which St Petersburg stands that was stored in a 10ft deep pit under the studio floor.

Anikushin was an important man when I met him, with a lot of influence in the city. He embraced Russian history and Soviet times, and often throughout the chaos of recent years I would find him sitting in his large high-backed chair with his head in his hands, sighing, 'Poor, poor Russia.' Of all the

locations in this book, this concrete studio with the grey northern light coming in through a vast, dusty window is where I discovered the most about the city of St Petersburg, and about what was happening in Russia.

LEFT: *'A busy person achieves everything!' Anikushin and Katya Galitzine working in the studio in 1992.*

RIGHT: *At the beginning of 1990, Anikushin was working on a statue of Chekhov – endless, elegant Chekhovs, in various stages of undress, leaning lazily against radiators, were scattered about the studio. Anikushin's Classical academic style was highly respected, despite the Soviet government's patronage of 'politically correct' Socialist Realism.*

LEFT: *Time stood still in this dusty place and yet Anikushin had an amazing ability to keep up with the changing times, working on public monuments and private commissions right through to his death in 1997. The studio has a scaffold for monuments, and a huge crane that lifted the little man to the top of a sculpture.*

233

46 FONTANKA

LEFT: *The Prince George Galitzine Memorial Library was created for the people of St Petersburg; it was to be one of the first libraries where readers could browse and choose books. For six months I worked with a local architect and builder, insisting on Russian wood for the shelves and parquet floors, and for a Classical ceiling with gently rounded corners instead of the harsh concrete that existed. I wanted to create a look that was 'Classical' but not so austere it would frighten people away.*

OPPOSITE PAGE BOTTOM: *My great-grandfather, who bought the house in 1895, was a great bibliophile, building the galleried Oak Library that held several thousand volumes. One of our most treasured possessions is an original Mecklenburg-Strelitz book with Duke George's ex libris, a green leather-bound tome which left Russia in 1920. It was inherited by my Uncle Emanuel, who donated it back to its original home in memory of his brother.*

For many years my father would pass his mother's family house on the Fontanka, longing to see inside. So many times he rang the bell, but he was always met with a stony-faced 'Nyet' from the Soviet guard on duty. 'But my mother lived here,' he would explain. In October 1994, two years after his death, my mother and I opened the Prince George Galitzine Memorial Library in the former Winter Garden, donated for this project by the present occupants of the building, the Mayakovsky Library. The theme of the Galitzine Library is 'Rossica' – a word invented by Russian scholars to cover books about Russia published abroad. Many such books were not allowed into Soviet Russia and we chose to fill the gap with books dating from 1917.

My great-grandmother, Natalia Vanlarskaya, was a lady-in-waiting to Grand Duchess Catherine Mikhailovna when young Duke George fell in love with her. He was refused permission to marry someone not of noble birth, and sent to Europe to get over his 'crush'. While he was away the Grand Duchess was visited in a dream by the Virgin Mary and told that her son would only be happy with Natalia, so George was called back and allowed to marry his mother's companion. It was a morganatic marriage, and Natalia was given the title of Countess Carlow from one of the family estates in the Ukraine. George chose 46 Fontanka as their home after the Michael Palace, which was too grand for a non-royal family, had been nominated by the Tsar as the new Russian Museum. Countess Carlow lived in the house – which was known as Dom Carlow – until 1920.

46 Fontanka is a house of love; it was filled with culture and music and the romantic dreams of three happy daughters and their baby brother. They were brought up with dignity, in a society that no longer exists. Those who emigrated took that dignity with them to their newly adopted countries. Our Library has a magical atmosphere, no doubt watched over by the souls of my father, in whose memory it was begun, and also my grandmother, Katya, and great-aunts, Merika and Tasha. It depends on donations to The Galitzine-St Petersburg Trust, a registered charity in both the UK and USA, and every month we have book presentations or lectures on appropriate themes. The White Hall, which was once filled with the melodies of a private quartet, now hosts passionate discussions on the authenticity of Romanov remains or reminiscences of exiled authors' lives. Russia has not given us back our heritage, instead we use the family house to bring some of Russia's missing heritage to them.

Of course the house is not mine, never will be, but I do feel a sense of belonging. It is the house of my ancestors and my mother and I have put in so much work that it is part of our family once more. Most of all I love to visit on a Sunday when it is empty, to read books in the sunlight streaming through the huge windows. On our anniversary we have a celebration – in 1997 we gave a concert and the sun's reflection off the Fontanka shimmered across the walls of the White Hall, creating ghostly shadows that could so easily have been the spirits of my family dancing for joy. The Library has been called 'a jewel', 'a Phoenix', 'a treasure' – it is all these things and within my heart something more: it is forgiveness, giving back what was taken away, both from the people of St Petersburg and my own family. It is peace.

ABOVE: *Detail of the painted ceiling in the Drawing Room, with a scene from one of the Mecklenburg-Strelitz estates. This room has a secret door leading to the Oak Library, and was part of the main enfilade leading to the White Hall.*

GLOSSARY

Akhmatova, Anna Andreevna (1889-1966) poetess popular in the early 1900s. In 1946 she was one of the chief targets in attempts to impose Party control over cultural life, but became active again after Stalin's death.

Badmaev, Peter Alexandrovich (1811-1920) healer, who treated Nicholas II for nerves. He was made a general before the Revolution, which led to his arrest by the Cheka in 1917. Hospital No. 23 is now the Badmaev centre of healing.

Bakst, Leon (pseudonym for Rosenburg, Lev Samuelovich) (1864-1924) painter and theatrical designer, who studied at the Academy of Arts in Paris and designed sets and costumes for the Ballets Russe. He used large splashes of intense colour and veered towards the exotic.

Baranovsky, Gabriel Vassilievich (1860-1920) civil engineer and official representative of the Technical Building Committee for the Ministry of Interior Affairs, who worked as an architectural advisor to other government departments. He was a specialist in construction laws and city planning, but also built many houses for the Eliseev family.

Barclay de Tolly, Mikhail Bogdanovich (1716-1818) Russian General Field Marshal of Scottish descent, famous for his march across the frozen Gulf of Finland in 1809. He commanded the Russian forces against Napoleon in 1812, but was replaced by Kutuzov.

Bazhenov, Vassily Ivanovich (1737-99) one of the great Russian architects, who studied in Moscow, St Petersburg, Paris and Rome. He fell into disfavour with Catherine the Great for supplying Masonic material to her son Paul, and much of his work was continued anonymously.

Bely, Andrei (pseudonym for Bugaev, Boris Nikolaevich) (1880-1934) poet, novelist, literary theorist and leader of the younger Symbolists. His work is obscure and difficult, being full of linguistic experiments.

Belorussia originally part of the Grand Duchy of Lithuania, Belorussia developed its own identity in the 13th and 14th centuries. Most Belorussians remained Russian and Orthodox when the Duchy entered into a union with Catholic Poland in 1569.

Benois, Alexander Nikolaevich (1870-1960) art historian and critic, who was a founder member of the artistic association *Mir Iskusstvo* (World of Art).

Benois, Leonti Nikolaevich (1856-1928) architect, who taught architecture at the Academy of Arts and encouraged the Renaissance style. His students included Lidval, Fomin, Lialevich, Peretiatkovich and Pokrovsky, all of whom favoured the Neo-classical style under his influence.

Benois, Nikolai Leontivich (1813-98) architect, who built the stable complex in English Gothic style at Peterhof, where he was Court Architect. He later became Chief Architect for the Emperor's theatres and Chairman of the St Petersburg Association of Architects. He was the father of Alexander and Leonti.

Benois, Yuli Yulievich (1852-1929) nephew of Alexander and Leonti Benois.

Berberova, Nina (1901-1993) moved in literary circles as a young girl, but emigrated after 1917. Taught Russian at Princeton, Yale and Colombia Universities. Her autobiography, *The Italics are Mine* (Knopf, New York, 1969) describes Russian literary life.

Bolshevik follower of a radical trend in Russian Social Democracy. When the Provisional Government was unable to provide leadership after the February Revolution, the Bolsheviks staged the October Revolution and seized power helped by the Red Guard.

Bolshoi Dom colloquial name for the KGB building in Leningrad.

Bonstedt, Ludwig Ludwigovich (1822-85) architect from a German merchant family.

Borovikovsky, Vladimir Lukich (1757-1825) Court artist, who became known as the Russian Gainsborough. His icon of St Catherine hangs in the Kazan Cathedral and he also painted many miniatures.

Bosse, Harold Andreevich (1812-94) architect and painter, who studied in Dresden and Darmstadt. He was Court Architect from 1858 and built several palaces in the country. He was a popular interior designer with the Russian gentry.

Boudry, David de (1756-1821) brother of Jean-Paul Marat, whose name was changed by Catherine the Great through fear of his brother's involvement in the French revolution. He was the teacher of French at the Lycée from 1811-21.

Boyars higher nobility, who headed civil and military administration and formed the major part of the Tsar's Council before the Romanov Dynasty. The Galitzines and the Dolgorukys were two of the oldest Boyar families.

Brodsky, Joseph (1940-1996) Russian poet, who won the Nobel prize for Literature in 1987.

Bryullov, Karl Pavlovich (1799-1852) painter who studied at the Academy of Arts and worked in Rome, where his gigantic historical painting, *The Last Day of Pompeii*, was painted.

Buchanan, Meriel (c1920) daughter of the British Ambassador to Russia during the 1917 Revolution, who wrote about events in St Petersburg in her book, *Petrograd: The City of Trouble 1914-1918* (Collins, London, 1918).

Bukharin, Nikolai Ivanovich (1888-1938) leading theorist of the Bolshevik Party. He returned to Russia after the February Revolution, playing a prominent part in preparations for the seizure of power. He later fell out with Stalin, was made chief defendant in a show trial and executed.

Cheka abbreviation for the Extraordinary Commission, the Soviet political police from 1917 to 1922. See also **NKVD, Okhrana** and **OMON**.

Chevakinsky, Savva Ivanovich (1713-74/80) distinguished exponent of the Baroque style in the mid-eighteenth century. Worked on part of the original interior of the Winter Palace as an assistant to Rastrelli and built the church at the Catherine Palace and St Nicholas Church.

Corsini, Geronimo Domenicovich (1808-76) designer of the gates for the Sheremetev Palace.

Custine, Marquis de (1790-1857) travelled to Russia in 1839 and later wrote *Letters from Russia* (1843), which was recognized as an accurate account of the Tsarist regime.

Decembrists a group of noblemen, dissatisfied with the autocracy of the Tsar, who planned a coup on the accession of Nicholas I in 1825. The revolt was badly organised, soldiers and officers were confused by different orders, peasants thought 'Konstitutsia' (constitution, in Russian) was the wife of Konstantin, the Tsar's brother. Five of the ringleaders were executed and more than 100 others sent to Siberia.

Deux Francais travelogue written in 1790-92, and published as *Voyage de deus Francai dans le Nord de l'Europe, 1790-92* (A de Fortia de Piles, Paris, 1796).

Diaghilev, Sergei Pavlovich (1872-1929) impresario, who put on concerts and exhibitions of Russian music and art in the West. He founded the Ballets Russe in Monte Carlo.

Diderot, Denis (1713-84) French man of letters and philosopher, who was chief editor of the *Encyclopedié* - one of the principal works of the Age of Enlightenment.

Dmitriev, Alexander Ivanovich (1878-1959) architect and academic, who was a professor at the Moscow Institute for Communal Buildings in Soviet times and was made a Doctor of Architecture in 1947.

Dmitriev, Grigory Dmitrievich (1714-46) assistant architect, who took over construction of the Anichkov Palace after Zemtsov's death in 1744. He carried out his master's plans with certain modifications.

Dokuchaev, Vassily Vassilievich (1846-1903) geologist, who was a professor at the St Petersburg University from 1883. He developed the sciences of genetic soil studies and zonal agronomy.

Dolgorukaya, Ekaterina (Katya) Mikhailovna (1847-1922) mistress of Alexander II and mother of three illegitimate children. She became Princess Yurievskaya in a highly secret ukase and in 1880 became Alexander's second wife.

Donchenko, Alexander Dmitrievich (1863-?) military engineer.

Esenin, Sergei Alexandrovich (1895-1925) poet, whose work was not accepted by the Soviet literary establishment although some of his poems later became popular songs. He married Isadora Duncan and they toured America and Europe, but the marriage did not last. In 1925 he hanged himself in Leningrad, causing a wave of sympathy suicides amongst cultural youth.

Fokine, Mikhail Mikhailovich (1880-1942) dancer and choreographer, who was influenced by Isadora Duncan and Siamese hand ballet and introduced many innovations to ballet.

Fomin, Ivan Alexandrovich (1872-1936) academician of architecture, graphic designer and craftsman of applied arts. Follower of Russian Classicism, and author, with I.E. Grabar, of *The History of Russian Art*. Chief Architect in Moscow from 1933 to 1936.

Fontana, Giovanni Mario (c1710) Italian architect, who came to Russia in 1703 and worked in St Petersburg and Moscow from 1711 to 1714/7. He is credited with the designs for the Menshikov palaces in St Petersburg (1710-27) and at Oranienbaum (1710-23), but there are several inconsistencies in the dates. There were also several other Fontanas working in St Petersburg, such as Francesco Fontana from 1710-12.

Fontana, Ludwig Franzevich (1824-94) academic architect who studied in Italy and was attested by the Academy of Arts in 1851. As well as the Grand Hotel Europe, he also designed for the Imperial Court and Ministry of Finance.

Gapon, George Apollonovich (1870-1906) Orthodox priest, who founded the Assembly of Russian Workers in St Petersburg in 1903 and led a procession of workers to present a petition to the Tsar on January 9, 1905. They were fired on and 'Bloody Sunday' started the 1905 uprising.

Gauger, Wilhem Karlovich (1847-1937) military engineer and specialist in ventilation techniques.

Glinka, Mikhail Ivanovich (1804-57) the first important Russian composer, whose influence on Russian music is as great as Pushkin's on poetry. His famous opera, *A Life for the Tsar* (1836), used adapted Russian folk tunes and opened the Imperial theatre season.

Glinka, Vassily Andreevich (1790-1830) architect, whose only known work in St Petersburg is on the Rumiantsev Palace.

Gogen, Alexander Ivanovich von (1856-1914) architect and applied artist, who was architect for the Ministry of War at the beginning of the twentieth century and was on the editorial council of *Architect* magazine.

Griboedev, Alexander Sergeevich (1798-1829) author famous for one great play, *Woe from Wit* (1823), a satirical comedy on Russian high society. He became minister-plenipotentiary to Persia in 1828 and was murdered during anti-Russian riots.

Herzen, Alexander Ivanovich (1812-70) founder of Russian populism and one of the country's earliest socialists. Published *The Bell* from 1857, but left Russia in the 1840s for political reasons.

Iofan, Dmitry Mikhailovich (1885-1961) one of the architects who won a competition to design the Main Treasury in 1912, and who worked on various buildings in the Kremlin after the Revolution.

Ivanov, Victor Mikhailovich (1846-?) military engineer and specialist in the building of barracks.

Kiev Rus a 9th-13th century state, ruled by princes – later Grand Princes – and situated on the trade routes from Scandinavia to Byzantium and from Western Europe to Central Asia. It was destroyed by the Mongol conquest of 1237-40.

Kitner, Geronimo Sebastianovich (1839-1929) academic architect, master of metal constructions, and, in 1868-1903, professor in the Builders' Faculty at the Institute of Civil Engineers. He later became a distinguished member of the Academy of Arts.

Klodt, Peter Karlovich (1805-67) sculptor of equestrian statues. His horses stand on the Anichkov bridge and he is also famous for his monument to Krylov in the Summer Garden and the equestrian statue of Nicholas I in St Isaac's Square.

Kolontai, Alexandra Mikhailovna (1872-1952) politician and theorist of 'free love'. From 1908 she lived abroad and was a member of the International Bureau of Women Socialists. After the February Revolution she was a member of the Bolshevik Central Committee and from 1923 she was a Soviet diplomat.

Korvin-Krukovsky, Sergei Sergeevich (1874-1937) one of the architects who won a competition to design the Main Treasury in 1912.

Kosyakov, George Antonovich (1872-1925) academician of architecture at the Academy of Arts, brother of Vassili and Vladimir.

Kosyakov, Vassily Antonovich (1862-1921) engineer and architect, who was architect for the Synod, and for the Imperial Court from 1910. Brother of Georgy and Vladimir.

Kosyakov, Vladimir Antonovich (1866-1922) engineer, architect and watercolourist. Brother of Georgy and Vladimir.

Kropotkin, Pyotr Alexandrovich (1842-1921) sociologist, geographer and geologist, who was also famous as a Revolutionary from the noble classes. He was arrested in 1874, but escaped to England. He lived in Switzerland and then France, but returned to Russia after 1917.

Krylov, Ivan Andreevich (1769-1844) satirical writer famous for moralistic animal fables.

Kutuzov, Mikhail Ilarionovich (1745-1813) Field marshal who commanded the Russian forces in the Russo-Turkish war in 1811 and the Patriotic War against Napoleon in 1812-13.

Lidval, Feodor Ivanovich (1870-1945) academic architect from 1909. Worked on projects in Moscow, Kiev, Kharkov, Astrakhan and Omsk, as well as in St Petersburg. Received many commissions from Alfred Noble and was popular with the Swedish community in St Petersburg. After 1918 he worked in Sweden.

Likhachev, Dmitry Sergeevich (1906-) graduate of Leningrad University, who was arrested in 1928 and sent to a camp. He became a Professor at Leningrad University between 1946-53. He supported the return of artefacts and archives removed from Russia during and after 1917, and is probably the most influential cultural figure of the Perestroika and Glasnost periods.

Lunacharsky, Anatoly Vassilievich (1873-1933) Marxist literary critic and politician from 1917-29. He was People's Commissar for Education for the USSR.

Lvov, Nikolai Alexandrovich (1751-1803) architect, artist and poet, who was a member of the Academy of Russia and the Academy of Arts. He was a leading exponent of Classicism in Russian architecture.

Lyall, Robert (1790-1831) botanist and traveller, who lived in St Petersburg in 1815 as a nobleman's physician and later travelled round Russia for several years.

Mayakovsky, Vladimir Vladimirovich (1893-1930) poet and leading Russian representative of the Futurist school. He worked for the Communist Party after the October Revolution and played an active role in propaganda campaigns. Disillusionment with the Party and misfortune in love drove him to suicide.

Melnikov, Abraham Ivanovich (1784-1854) architect, who worked in the late Classical style and was involved in the planning of St Isaac's Cathedral.

Meltzer, Roman Feodorovich (1860-1943) architect and specialist in applied arts, chief designer and co-owner of the furniture firm, F. Meltzer & Co. He decorated interiors in the Anichkov, Alexander, Catherine and Winter Palaces, and designed the railings and gates that were around the Winter Palace before the Revolution.

Menshikov, Alexander Danilovich (1673-1729) a poor stable boy, he rose to become a statesman, field marshal and prince as Peter the Great's powerful right hand man. He ruled Russia during the reign of Catherine I and the minority of Peter II, but was later banished to Siberia.

Mesmakher, Maximilian Yegorovich (1842-1906) Russian architect of German descent, an outstanding draughtsman whose architectural drawings are in the Hermitage and who created particularly sumptuous interiors.

Meyer, Christian (c1750) gifted Russian cabinet-maker, of German origin, who was active in St Petersburg in the last quarter of the 18th century. He was previously attributed as a pupil of David Roentgen (1743-1807), but is now thought to have been working in St Petersburg before 1783. His work stood in many of the major Imperial palaces.

Meyerhold, Vsevolod Emilievich (1874-1942) outstanding actor and director, a gifted and extreme modernistic innovator. He fell foul of Stalin, was arrested in 1939 and disappeared.

Monighetti, Ippolito (1819-78) Russian architect of Italian descent. His buildings in St Petersburg are mainly in Baroque or early Neo-classical style.

Nashchokin, Pavel Voinovich (1801-54) friend and penpal of Pushkin, who lived in Moscow.

NEP abbreviation for the New Economic Policy practised by the Bolshevik Government in 1921-8, which aimed to restore the economy by making concessions to private enterprise in agriculture, trade and industry.

NKVD abbreviation for the People's Commissariat of Internal Affairs, the Soviet security service from 1934-43. In 1943 it was split into two commissariats, the NKVD and the NKGB, the latter having responsibility for State security and later becoming the MGB and then the KGB. See also **Cheka, Okhrana** and **OMON**.

Novikov, Nikolai Ivanovich (1744-1818) writer, journalist and publisher, who was dedicated to enlightening Russia. His magazine *The Drone* made fun of Catherine the Great's journal, *This and That* and was closed down in 1770. His later satirical journals, *Empty Chat* (1770), *The Painter* (1772-3) and *The Purse* (1774) were also all closed.

October Revolution seizure of power by the Bolsheviks on the 7th November 1917 (25th October Old Style). A new government was established with Lenin at its head.

Okhrana colloquial name of the security police before 1917. Liberal opinion regarded its activities as vicious, but it did work within strict legal norms. It was abolished by the Provisional Government after the February Revolution. See also **Cheka, NKVD** and **OMON**.

Old Believers large sect which separated from the Russian Orthodox Church in the 17th century because they refused to recognise the service books as edited and corrected by Patriarch Nikon. Until the middle of the 19th century they were persecuted by the State.

OMON stands for Otryad Militia Osobogo Naznacheniya, or the Special Police Squad. See also **Cheka, NKVD** and **Okhrana**.

Ordzhonikidze, Grigory Konstantinovich (1886-1937) politician, one of Lenin's close Bolshevik associates during the Revolution and a member of Stalin's Politburo from 1930. Committed suicide in 1937 at the time of the great repressions.

Palekh village in south Russia where they have continued the tradition of painting lacquer boxes throughout the centuries to the present day. The Palekh style of painting is quite distinctive.

People's Will, The (sometimes translated as People's Freedom) populist revolutionary organization formed in 1879, which assassinated government representatives. After the murder of Alexander II most of the leaders were arrested, but the organization continued to exist in small groups. The St Petersburg group, led by Lenin's brother, Alexander Ulianov, attempted the assassination of Alexander III.

Petipa, Marius (1822-1910) French choreographer and teacher, who came to St Petersburg in 1847. He changed the course of Russian ballet, introducing new steps, high quality music and coalescing French Classical ballet with Italian acrobatics.

Petrashevsky Circle founded by Mikhail Butashevich-Petrashevsky (1821-66), son of a nobleman doctor and political dissident. In 1849 Petrashevsky was arrested for Revolutionary activities sent to Siberia. In 1860 he began the radical newspaper *Amor*.

Petrogradsky side or area one of the main islands on which St Petersburg is built.

Pimenov, Stepan Stepanovich (1784-1833) wood sculptor and academician, who worked with architects in St Petersburg in the early 19th century and also made figurines for the Imperial Porcelain Factory.

Politburo chief policy-making organ of the Communist Party until 1991. The first Politburo was formed on the eve of the October Revolution and was made permanent in 1919. In 1952 it temporarily became the Presidium of the Central Committee, but later reverted to its former name.

Pomerantsev, Alexander Nikanorovich (1849-1918) academic and professor of architecture. Rector of the Academy of Arts 1899-1900, and specialist in the building of schools.

Potemkin, Grigory Alexandrovich (1739-91) statesman, and favourite of Catherine the Great. In 1787 he erected fake villages in New Russia as Catherine travelled past so she would believe it more populated and prosperous – hence the term 'Potemkin villages', which arose after his death. He developed the Caucasus and the south of Russia.

Prokofiev, Ivan Prokofievich (1758-1828) gilder and sculptor, who studied in Paris and Berlin and became an academician. He worked with Voronikhin.

Prospekt avenue.

Pshenitzky, Andrei Petrovich (?) engineer, who moved to Poland in 1920 and became Rector of Warsaw Polytechnic.

Pushchin, Ivan Ivanovich (1798-1859) Decembrist, son of a Senator and a contemporary of Pushkin.

Quarenghi, Giacomo (1744-1817) Italian architect admired and patronised by Catherine the Great. He came to St Petersburg in 1779 and designed many famous buildings around the city, working in an elegant Neo-classical style.

Rakhau, Karl Karlovich (1830-80) academic and professor of architecture, who was senior town architect from 1871.

Rasputin, Grigory Yefimovich (1872-1916) uneducated Siberian peasant, who apparently saved the life of the haemophiliac Tsarevich on several occasions and so had a strong hold on the Empress during the last years of the Romanovs. He was murdered by Felix Yusupov; after surviving being poisoned and shot, his body was thrown into the Moika and he drowned.

Rastrelli, Francesco Bartolomeo (1700-1771) Italian architect who came to Russia in 1716 with his father, Carlo Bartolomeo. He was the leading exponent of the Baroque style and a favourite architect of Empress Elizabeth. His major buildings include the Catherine Palace, the Winter Palace and Smolny Cathedral and Convent.

Repin, Ilya Yefimovich (1844-1930) painter and accomplished 19th century realist, a prolific and versatile Russian artist after whom the Academy of Arts was renamed in Soviet times.

Rimsky-Korsakov, Nikolai Andreevich (1844-1908) composer, whose work is elegant and exuberant, although sometimes repetitious. Most of his operas are based on national subjects and are full of folk music.

Rinaldi, Antonio (1709-94) Italian architect invited to Russia by Count Kyril Razumovsky in 1752. Some of his important works include the Chinese Palace at Oranienbaum, Gatchina and the Marble Palace. His style bridged the transition from Baroque to Neo-classicism.

Rochefort, Nikolai Ivanovich de (1846-1905) engineer architect who worked in the technical section of the Ministry of the Interior in 1866-88 and 1889-97 and was involved in the planning and building of the railway networks in Russia.

Rossi, Carlo Ivanovich (1775-1849) architect of Italian origin, brought up in Russia. He was chief architect to Alexander I and played a major part in creating the great Classical architectural ensembles of St Petersburg.

RSFSR Russian Soviet Federative Socialist Republic, official name of the largest and most economically important Union Republic of the USSR.

Rublev, Andrei (1360-1430) icon painter, who combined an understanding of late Greek art with distinctive draughtsmanship and a genius for composition. His serene *Trinity* is widely known in reproduction, and has never been surpassed in its expression of exalted emotion.

Rusca, Luigi (1758-1822) Swiss architect, who lived in St Petersburg from 1783 and worked on the Tauride, Anichkov and Strelna palaces. He published a famous collection of engravings showing his projects.

Saltykov-Shchedrin, Mikhail Yevgrafovich (1826-89) satirical writer who worked for the government, was banished and later retired as vice-governor of a province to devote himself to literature. He was co-editor of *The Contemporary*, and edited its successor, *The Notes of the Fatherland*.

Samokhvalov, Vladimir Petrovich (1846-c1916) worked in Yaroslav until 1875, and was an architect in St Petersburg for the Palace Department, 1875-92.

scagliola imitation stone or marble, made of pulverized selenite applied to a wet gesso ground, fixed under heat and highly polished. It can match genuine stone, or come in unusual colours such as pink or blue.

Schlüter, Andreas (1659-1714) distinguished sculptor and architect, who worked mainly in Germany. He came to St Petersburg in 1713, where he stayed until he died.

Scotti, Giovanni Battista (1776-1830) artist, who was born in Italy and came to St Petersburg with his father, Carlo Scotti, in 1786. He was a master of monumental Classical paintings, and his work is in many palaces, including Pavlovsk and the Michael Palace.

Serafimov, Sergei Savvich (1878-1939) one of the architects who won a competition to design the Main Treasury in 1912.

Shchedrin, Apollon Fedoseevich (1796-1847) academic architect and professor at the Academy of Arts. Worked with Rossi on the Public Library.

Shevchenko, Taras Grigorevich (1814-61) Ukrainian poet, who was banished from St Petersburg in 1847 and forbidden to write or paint for ten years for belonging to a secret society, the Brotherhood of Saints Kyril and Methodius. On his release, he lived in St Petersburg.

Smith, Hedrick (1933-) veteran *New York Times* correspondent, who won the Pulitzer Prize in 1974 for coverage of Moscow. He wrote *The Russians*, later updated to *The New Russians* (Times Books, London, 1976).

Socialist Realism basic method of literature and art, conceived by Stalin, Zhdanov and Gorky as a development of Lenin's 'partyness of literature'.

Sokolov, Yegor Timofeevich (1750-1824) academic architect and master of Classicism. He supervised the reconstruction of the Marble Palace, Anichkov Palace, Gatchina, Pavlovsk and supervised the construction of the Alexander Palace, among many other projects.

Stakenschneider, Andrei Ivanovich (1802-65) talented Russian architect, of German descent, who designed many fine buildings in St Petersburg. He also introduced several technical innovations in building design in Russia.

Stanislavsky, Konstantin Sergeevich (1863-1938) great actor and director. In 1898 he founded the Moscow Art Theatre, famous for its productions of Chekhov and Gorky. He developed the Stanislavsky technique, based on the realist tradition in the Russian theatre. His book, *An Actor Prepares* (1936) has influenced modern acting technique in Russia and abroad.

Starov, Ivan Yegorovich (1744-1808) architect and master of the Classical style, which he reduced to simple and severe forms. His colonnaded hall in the Tauride Palace set the fashion for columns in Russian interiors.

Stasov, Vassily Petrovich (1769-1848) Classical architect, whose main buildings are the Court Stables and Church, the Ismailovsky Regiment Trinity Cathedral and the Moscow Triumphal Gates. He also decorated the interior of Smolny Cathedral, disregarding Rastrelli's Baroque exterior.

Stepanov, Alexander Alexandrovich (1856-1913) architect on the committee 'Looking After Beggars', who also redesigned the interiors of the Rumiantsev Palace and the Yusupov Palace on the Moika.

Stolypin, Peter Arkadievich (1862-1911) statesman who carried out a dual policy of firm suppression of the revolution of 1905, while implementing reforms to remove the causes of discontent. He was assassinated in 1911 at the Kiev Opera House, by a Socialist Revolutionary terrorist who was also a police agent.

Suvorov, Count Alexander Vassilievich (1730-1800) Generalissimo, the greatest Russian soldier, who distinguished himself in the Seven Years War and the Russo-Turkish wars. In 1798 he defeated the French in a series of brilliant attacks and conquered northern Italy.

Svinin, Vassily Feodorovich (1865-1939) official architect for the Academy of Arts and the Russian Museum between 1895 and 1897.

Tamansky, Peter Ivanovich (1806-83) architect, who also worked in Moscow and Perm. He was architect for the Engineering Department and teacher at the main Engineering College of St Petersburg from 1837 to 1853.

Thomon, Thomas de (1754-1813) leading Neo-classical architect in Russia, who was born in Berne and studied in Paris and Rome. He arrived in St Petersburg in 1789 and became Court Architect to Alexander I.

Trezzini, Domenico (1670-1734) Swiss architect, one of the first foreign architects to come to Russia at the invitation of Peter the Great. He was very active in the early construction of St Petersburg.

Tributs, Admiral Vladimir Filipovich (1900-77) Commander of the Baltic Fleet during the Second World War.

Trotsky, Lev Davidovich (1879-1940) Jewish politician, who joined the Social Democratic movement in 1896. He played a leading role in the 1905 revolution and was one of Lenin's chief supporters after the February Revolution. He fell foul of Stalin, was expelled from Russia and murdered by Soviet agents in Mexico City.

Tsar title of the rulers of Muscovy from the 15th century, until Peter the Great assumed the title Emperor of All Russia. The title of Tsar was still widely used throughout the imperial period.

Tsarskoe Selo town just south of St Petersburg, literally translated as Tsar's Village. The name derives from Saritsa, the name of an ancient settlement on the site. The name became Sarskoe Selo when the Russians took control of the area in Peter the Great's time, and then officially Tsarskoe Selo in 1808. After the 1917 Revolution, the name was changed to Detskoe Selo (Children's Village), and then to Pushkin in 1937 to mark the centennial of the poet's death. It is now known as Tsarskoe Selo once more.

Ulitsa street.

Vakhtangov, Evgeny Bagrationovich (1883-1922) actor and producer of Armenian origin, a pupil of Stanislavsky. He belonged to the Moscow Art Theatre from 1911. His Third Studio, where he produced modern mystery plays, was renamed the Vakhtangov Theatre in 1926.

Vallin de la Mothe, Jean-Baptiste (1729-1801) architect who came to Russia in 1759 and taught architecture at the newly-founded St Petersburg Academy of Arts. He was a pioneer of the Neo-classical style and he designed several buildings in the city. He left Russia in 1776.

Vekshinsky, Alexander Nikolaevich (1859-1908) academic architect, who was town architect in Pskov, 1886-88, and professor and teacher at the Academy of Arts and teacher at the Electric Institute in St Petersburg.

Velten, Yuri Matveevich (1730-1801) architect, whose most well-known masterpieces are Chesme Church, built to celebrate the Russian fleet's victory over the Turks in 1770 at the Bay of Chesma, and the railings for the Summer Garden.

Vladimir, Great Prince (Vladimir I) (956-1015) patron saint of Russian Christians and Grand Prince of Kiev from 980.

Voeykov, Alexander Ivanovich (1842-1916) meteorologist, geographer and climatologist. He was President of the Commission for the Russian Geographical Society, and also worked abroad as a meteorologist in the USA, Canada, Japan, Mexico and Chile.

Voronikhin, Andrei Nikiforovich (1760-1814) Russian architect, one of the leading exponents of the Neo-classical style in St Petersburg. He began life as a serf on the land of Alexander Stroganov.

Wrangel, Piotr Nikolaevich (1878-1928) general who served in the Russo-Japanese War and the First World War. He joined the anti-Bolshevik forces in 1918 and held out the longest, until he was forced to retreat and evacuated from Sevastopol in 1920.

ZAGS stands for Zapis Aktov Grazhdansogo Sostoyaniya, or Civil Records Department.

Zemstvo colloquial name of the local government institutions established in 1864, with authority in economic and educational matters, and areas such as public health. This was widened after the February Revolution, but they were abolished after the October Revolution and replaced by the soviets.

Zemtsov, Mikhail Grigorievich (1688-1743) one of the founding architects of St Petersburg, who helped to create the city's outline at the beginning of the 1730s.

Zhukovsky, Vassily Andreevich (1783-1852) poet and translator, who was a friend of Pushkin and Glinka. He introduced the narrative ballad to Russia by translating Sir Walter Scott and others, and later wrote his own as well as the words for Glinka's opera, *A Life for the Tsar*.

Zinoviev, Grigory Yevseevich (1883-1936) Jewish politician, member of the Social Democratic Labour Party from 1901 and a Bolshevik from 1903. In the conflict after Lenin's death he changed sides several times. Sentenced to ten years' imprisonment in 1935 for his involvement in the assassination of Kirov, he was tried again in the show trials of 1936 and executed.

INDEX